JOHN KEATS
THE PRINCIPLE OF BEAUTY

JOHN KEATS:
THE PRINCIPLE OF BEAUTY

BY LORD GORELL

HASKELL HOUSE PUBLISHERS Ltd.
Publishers of Scarce Scholarly Books
NEW YORK. N. Y. 10012
1970

First Published 1948

HASKELL HOUSE PUBLISHERS LTD.
Publishers of Scarce Scholarly Books
280 LAFAYETTE STREET
NEW YORK, N. Y. 10012

Library of Congress Catalog Card Number: 72-122978

Standard Book Number 8383-1110-5

Printed in the United States of America

CONTENTS

I — AS IT WAS — 9

II — SUNRISE — 31

III — MORNING GLORY — 56

IV — SUNSET — 84

V — AS IT IS — 108

I — BIOGRAPHY IN BRIEF — 118

II — BOOKS — 120

III — INDEX — 122

THIS book was first begun at the request of the publishers; but it very speedily became a labour of love – and I stress both words. It has entailed labour of a more intense kind than any except endeavour to engage in original poetic creation; and I have loved every hour of the many spent upon it. It has given me pain to differ profoundly from a critic so attached and so eminent as Mr J. Middleton Murry; but the extent and vehemence of his imaginative, unsubstantiated rangings of assault upon Keats's love have left me no alternative. I have written only what I am convinced is truth – and that after a lifetime of thought and devotion.

I will only add this: there is but one recommendation to make to all who really want to know what manner of man Keats was, what he thought, what he felt, what he stood for, what he attempted, and what he achieved, and that is: do not pay overmuch attention to explanations and commentaries, but read his Letters, read his Poems; it is all there for everyone to understand and enjoy. He is simple, natural, modest, and great – four qualities very seldom combined: and he gives himself freely to all who seek, even as he loved, 'the principle of Beauty in all things'.

1948					GORELL

❦ I ❧
AS IT WAS

IN THE small hours of the morning of April 17, 1804, a popular, energetic man, thirty years of age, the owner-manager of some livery stables a little way down the road, was found by the night-watchman lying seriously injured in the City Road, Finsbury, opposite the Methodist Chapel, and he died a few hours later: it was supposed that he had been thrown from his horse on his way to his house in Craven Street; years later it was said, without evidence, that he had been engaged in undue conviviality with friends and was returning home, intoxicated: 'a man utterly free from vulgarity', he was called by a dispassionate witness. As far as is known, he had never had even a nodding acquaintance with writers, but his death profoundly affected literature in this country and indeed in the world. He left a widow, a lively, high-spirited girl, Frances, the daughter of those who had before he married been her husband's employers, Mr and Mrs Jennings: she was overcome with grief at her sudden loss, but rallied with sufficient celerity to be married again just over two months later, on June 27, choosing for her second marriage to William Rawlings the same church as she had had for her first, which had been to Thomas Keats. She had had five children by her first marriage; one boy, Edward, had died in infancy, three boys and one girl remained: of these the eldest, John, had been born on October 31, 1795, the youngest, Frances Mary (Fanny) on June 3, 1803. The death of Thomas Keats and his widow's remarriage broke up the home completely: the four children went to live with their grandparents, but Mr Jennings died the following year, Mrs Rawlings who had separated from her second husband rejoined her mother and her children and died in March, 1810; and Mrs Jennings then, before dying herself in 1814, placed the four children and their money in the charge of two trustees, Richard Abbey and John Rowland Sandell, merchants.

It is necessary briefly to restate these facts for two reasons. First, because of the quite astonishing inaccuracy with which they have been recorded even as recently as in two books, one published in 1934 and the other in 1936, and, secondly, because they are fundamental: they governed, and in two cases destroyed, the lives of the children. This would be of no consequence to the world but for one further fact, namely, that the eldest boy happened to be 'the greatest inheritor of unfulfilled renown' ever to exist.

Life, as most of us come to know, is a tapestry of vicissitudes, misprisions, paradoxes, and surprises: around few both in his days on earth and in his memories have these clustered in more abundance than around the eldest son of Thomas and Frances Keats. When he died of consumption in the Piazza di Spagna, Rome, on February 23, 1821, in the twenty-sixth year of his age, he was little known beyond the circle of his personal friends, so little known that he himself desired as a suitable epitaph the embittered sentence, 'His name was writ in water', and had written earlier his conviction that if he lived he would have made his name remembered, evincing a consciousness then of lack of recognition – though it must be added that for so young a writer he had, in fact, succeeded in making quite a mark which would assuredly, had he been spared to continue his literary career, have won him wide, and indeed enduring, recognition within a very short space of time.

He was not so spared, and he accordingly died still little known: only one of his friends was with him, a devoted painter by the name of Joseph Severn. He died abroad in severely straightened circumstances, a licensed apothecary who had abandoned that profession four and a half years before, as soon, in fact, as ever he had gained his licence, in order to embrace the precarious adventure of poetic endeavour: he had published three slender volumes – which in itself is some achievement at so early an age; but none had been financially successful. He left behind him a number of unpublished poems and many letters, to his friends, to his brother and sister-in-law in America, to his sister, and to the girl to whom he had been engaged to be married: he left also – legacies of which he may within his own consciousness have had an inkling but to which the facts could give no sort of rational support – an imperishable name, an honoured place high amidst the seats of the immortals, and, over and above these, around him both a love and a knowledge as warm and as close as, if not actually warmer and closer than, any around anyone who has ever passed along the vale of Life.

And here it may be remarked that it is generally assumed, as a complete matter of course, that every one in any way connected with a young genius so famous should naturally treasure every little scrap of paper that had on it any writing from his pen. That, obviously, is judgment after the event of the kind from which Keats and his love and his friends have suffered so much. It is surely a very remarkable thing that so many people carefully treasured the letters of this their brother or their friend, treasured them not merely at

JOHN KEATS: THE PRINCIPLE OF BEAUTY

the time of receipt and for a year or two afterwards but for years and years after his death – long after it seemed possible that their belief in his gaining that fame for which in his lifetime they had confidently hoped would ever be justified. Moreover, these treasured pieces of paper, letters and poems, were not held up to ransom in the days when their value became high: they were freely given, so that all honour might be done to their creator. It is unusual and it is fine – fully in accord with the character of the man concerned.

So it is that there is little or nothing that the world, if it chooses, cannot now know about the acts, the thoughts, the writings, the love – the movements both of the mind and of the heart – of John Keats. Every detail of importance has now come to light – which makes the ignorance still displayed almost inexcusable. In particular, perhaps, it is strange that commentators, those to whom, obviously, Keats meant, and means, so much and who have studied his life most closely, should in several instances be those who have poured scorn, very unjustly and very inaccurately, upon the two people who were most loved by him, namely, the two Fannys, Fanny Keats, his sister, and Fanny Brawne, to whom, had health been granted to him, he would, beyond any shadow of doubt, have been married – and happily married.

Fanny Keats has suffered much in the estimation of the world by reason of a chance encounter in Rome forty years after her brother's death, with F. Locker-Lampson. Her feelings were of the deepest, her memories of the most tenacious: his 'sprightliness', he said himself, 'made her yawn' which disappointed him but does not surprise us: she was not one to unburden herself gushingly to an impertinent, loquacious stranger. On December 3, 1881, more, that is, than sixty years after John Keats died, she wrote to H. Buxton Forman, to whose tact, devotion and scholarship in his editorial and literary labours every lover of Keats is greatly beholden, 'you can now more than ever understand my devotion to him who was all the world to me' – how many sisters can truthfully write so of a brother so long lost, sisters happily married with children of their own and living far from all they had known in youth? Fanny's whole story shows that in her words she was truthful. Of her Professor B. Ifor Evans, writing as recently as 1934, says, in unquestioning repetition of the superficial ignorance of Locker-Lampson, 'she grew into a fat, blonde, lymphatic woman, married to a Spanish man of letters, Valentin Llanos, and sharing apparently but little of the temperament of her brothers'. No biographer or commentator should write 'apparently' without verification: in this case the statement is beyond measure unjust.

It is to the steadfast remembrance and loving care of Fanny Keats that we owe so much of our knowledge of the tenderness of her great brother's mind: without her forty-eight of his letters—'the only collection in existence of a series of original letters of Keats written to one person' – would have perished and the story of their preservation for years and years is one of the most touching in literature and, though now set down in full by Marie Adami, at first in her two articles in the Cornhill Magazine for October 1935 and February 1936 and then in her *Fanny Keats* published in 1937, one of the least known. It is as deserving of immortality as the Letters themselves.

In December, 1935, it so fell out that I was privileged to be the first Englishman for a great number of years to be

JOHN KEATS: THE PRINCIPLE OF BEAUTY

allowed to hold in my hand that wonderful lock of hair which, having been preserved with such loving care for more than a century in Madrid, was brought back by Marie Adami as a gift to the British nation from Keats's grand-niece, Senora Elena Brockman — even as in March, 1891, forty-four of the precious letters had, through the agency of Mr H. Buxton Forman, been given by Rosa Llanos, Keats's niece. Much moved, I then wrote some lines as a tribute to Keats and to Fanny, the conclusion of which runs:

> is it not a truth
> That even the hurrying hordes must understand
> 'The principle of Beauty in all things'
> Outlasts mortality? This lock of hair,
> By love long tended in a foreign land,
> Comes home at length, an English heritage.
> O breathe on England's spirit in this hour
> And in the after-time to be to you
> The peace of Beauty that is fallen like dew
> Beyond the night upon your deathless day!
> Let this rich hair, this late returning dower
> Be for a blessing on the chequered way:
> A gift remote from Earth's regality,
> Simplicity its chaplet, may it be
> A wave-washed vessel with all peace imbued,
> A laying on of hands, a quietude,
> A cadenced murmur like a vesper bell,
> A truth deep sparkling in a dateless well;
> And down the avenue of ages prove
> The lasting radiance of a sister's love.

This was the second of the two small, personal experiences in direct connexion with John Keats that it has been my happy fortune to have: the first will be recorded in its due place.

'More than a century after her brother's death, nearly half a century after her own', Marie Adami wrote this inscription in respect of Fanny Keats in my private, specially bound reprint of the two Cornhill articles, *Fanny Keats and her Letters* – 'The sisters of great poets have sometimes lived within the circle of their brothers' fame, and have contributed to it themselves. This cannot be said of Fanny, the only sister of John Keats, but although until to-day interest and inquiry have passed her by, if affection brought others within those circles, and was the spring and source of their contribution, Fanny Keats belongs to their company'.

It is a modest epitaph, one that would have strongly appealed to her – and to Keats. Peace be to Fanny – peace and justice! Fat she may have become by 1861, blonde she may have been, lymphatic she was never. It is indeed a joy to all lovers of Keats to know, beyond all question, that throughout the whole of her long life – and she lived until December 16, 1889 – his only sister fully deserved the love he had shown towards her in her rather unhappy, circumscribed childhood and was in all respects worthy of his greatness. She was no poet herself, but she was out of the same mould as he – nor were her daughters and grandchildren less faithful to his memory.

As the first Fanny owed so long a period of misprision to the mis-termed *Confidences* of F. Locker-Lampson which gave the description under which she suffered in the public estimation until 1937, when the real truth about her was revealed, so – with a difference – has the second Fanny, Fanny Brawne, suffered, owing the length of her misprision

JOHN KEATS: THE PRINCIPLE OF BEAUTY

largely to the egocentricity of an American, Mr F. Holland Day, to whom in 1891 Rosa Llanos entrusted the thirty-one letters written to her mother, Fanny Keats, by Fanny Brawne. He took them to America and there secreted them: their existence was not so much as suspected until 1924 when Miss Amy Lowell, to the anger of Mr Day, who had apparently allowed her to look at them, quoted a few passages from them in her biography of Keats. Nothing more was allowed to be revealed until 1934 when, on their owner's death, they were bequeathed as a tardy act of reparation to the Keats Memorial House, Hampstead: even then it was made a condition that the gift should be regarded as anonymous – so much so that Mr F. Edgcumbe, then resident Curator of the Memorial House, did not feel himself at liberty when editing the letters at long last in 1936, to say more than that 'the letters have had a chequered history' and 'after many vicissitudes they came back to the house where they had originally been written'. The simple truth is they were kept by Fanny Keats till her death in 1889 and then in 1891 given as stated above.

Their importance is that they completely restablish Fanny Brawne, who had been so grievously traduced not only by one or two friends of Keats such as Charles Wentworth Dilke, but by the feelings roused by the publication in 1878 of Keats's letters to her: Sir Charles Dilke did not then hesitate to describe this in an article in the *Athenaeum* as 'this hideous breach of the sanctities of life' – but dispassionate opinion has not agreed with him: Keats and his life belong to the world. At all events, and whatever the poignancy and distress of Keats's letters in illness written to her, 'her letters to Keats's sister written after his death settle once and for all', so writes Marie Adami in her *Fanny*

AS IT WAS

Keats, 'the question of the sincerity of her affection and they enable us to judge also the depth of her understanding. It is just to remember that she knew Keats only in physical and in mental strain, for they first met when Tom's illness was far advanced, and when the disease from which John was to suffer had already begun its course.'

Justice is the last thing that either Fanny has had until recently, and some of the attacks on Fanny Brawne have gone as far from generosity as truth. Mr J. Middleton Murry, for instance in a very clever but so imaginative an analysis of the mind and thought of a poet that it passes often from factual exposition into the realms of fiction, his *Keats and Shakespeare*, published in 1925, not only sees her everywhere in Keats's writing, in places where she has never been seen before or since, but actually speaks of her as having 'the arch voice of the suburban belle'. Prejudice could hardly go further, but it does, as when Mr Murry writes categorically that 'Fanny Brawne killed Keats', a statement the more unjust because there is just this substratum of truth in it, that if Keats had not fallen so passionately in love with Fanny Brawne – or, let it be added, with any other girl whatsoever – it is conceivable that the illness which so consumed him that at his post mortem his lungs were found to be almost entirely destroyed, might have been fought a little more successfully: in the then state of medical ignorance that is most unlikely but it is just conceivable. In this way, and in this way only, was Fanny Brawne responsible for Keats's fate and yet Mr Murry can write 'as surely as any hero of humanity, he died for the truth that was in him': that really has no truth at all.

As to Fanny Brawne, there is nothing to be preferred to the direct and simple sentence of Professor Ifor Evans, in counter-balance to his unfairness to Fanny Keats: 'nothing', he wrote, 'has been more unjust than the condemnation under which she has suffered'. Miss Dorothy Hewlett's summary in her careful biography, *Adonais,* is 'the fine sensible girl we now know Fanny to have been, would not have failed Keats. One thing is abundantly clear; she loved him with her whole heart'. Also can be added the sober judgment of Mr Maurice Buxton Forman, in that great edition of Keats's letters which so splendidly carries on and completes the labours of his father, 'I am not among those who think otherwise than kindly and respectfully of her. I fully believe that she was warmly attached to Keats and mourned his loss long and bitterly' – a judgment the more valuable since it was pronounced in 1930, before the publication of the confirmatory letters of Fanny Brawne to Fanny Keats. Sportive and merry, even in the earlier passages flippant she was, but it is now indubitable that she was a true and tender-hearted girl who, together with her mother, was infinitely kind to, and understanding of, the young poet who loved her so feverishly, so jealously. She was all that he needed to make him a loving and helpful wife and that she was ready to become – but it was not to be. There let her rest.

It is indeed a strange fact that many who have most loved and praised John Keats not merely for his poems and his letters but for his character and understanding should have come to think so disparagingly of those with whose lives his was closest cast and who meant the most to him. His sister, his love, and one at least of his most intimate friends, Charles Armitage Brown, his companion in Scotland, his room-mate and his collaborator, are all tilted at – and worse. Brown was a bit of a flirt, he was exact in financial

AS IT WAS

dealings rather than generous, and his matrimonial experience was peculiar, but to set him down as a selfish, cold-blooded sensualist is unquestionably to set out to prove that Keats was an extraordinarily poor judge of people – far, in fact, from being 'one of the wisest of spirits'. It is necessary to state positively that very few men – certainly very, very few young, impoverished, ill men – have ever had such devoted friends as John Keats – and this to his last breath. Even Joseph Severn has been accused of climbing to distinction upon the memory of Keats; but if ever a man showed devotion to another it was Severn to Keats in the agonizing winter of 1820–21, even to braving the displeasure of a father, so irrational and extreme as to knock Severn down to try to prevent his going to Italy with his dying friend.

What is necessary in all these remembrances is not merely justice but also commonsense: post-factum verdicts are usually so dreadfully lacking in both qualities. Keats, it must be very plainly asserted, was not – either in his lifetime or for many years after his death – a famous man, still less a beloved world figure. He was a young, impecunious, high-spirited boy, in many ways difficult – as genius always is, particularly when allied to, or handicapped by, the seeds of consumption. To demand that his contemporaries should have dealt with him as – perhaps – he would have been dealt with if recreated in our midst to-day is to demand the wholly unreasonable. Yet this demand is always made in respect of his guardian, Richard Abbey. No commentator – not one – has a good word to say for Abbey; even Marie Adami, most exact and most judicial of writers, is without that. Let us, however, above all else, endeavour to be fair – even to him.

On March 20, 1810, Frances Rawlings died and in July

Mrs Jennings, her mother and grandmother to her four surviving children, appointed two merchants to be their trustees and guardians, Richard Abbey and John Rowland Sandell. These, obviously, were not appointed without their consent, but there has never been a word of criticism or disapprobation of Sandell, only of Abbey – yet Abbey did, or tried to do, what he conceived to be his duty; Sandell, as far as is known, did not. Mrs Jennings died in December, 1814: there is extant a rather amusing, stiff little testimonial signed 'J. S.' and dated January 14, 1816, to the effect that Fanny Keats had been 'a very good girl' during the time she was on a visit to Mr Sandell. So that he cannot have been totally neglectful or unmindful of the youngest at least of his charges. But beyond that single instance there is no evidence that he bothered about any of them in the slightest degree: and it is known that in 1816, owing to financial difficulties, he left England for Holland and that he died there in 1817.

At all events Richard Abbey, who had assumed control of the destinies and fortunes of the four children from July, 1810, onwards, was left by Mrs Jennings's death in indisputably sole control. After Keats's death George, who married Georgiana Wylie and died in Kentucky, to which he had long emigrated, in 1842, wrote to his sister Fanny in 1822, describing Abbey as 'that good man', even as he had previously called him 'that excellent man'. There is little to substantiate the excellency, and goodness is not the virtue that Abbey seemed to John, Tom, or Fanny to possess: but he was certainly not what he has since been painted. His wife was an ignorant, gabbling, narrow-minded woman, but there is no evidence she was ever actually unkind: Abbey himself was pompous, self-satisfied, and suspicious, but he had a very difficult responsibility and he fulfilled it to the best of his ability. 'No man', as Marion Crawford wrote of Venice and Venetian History, 'is to be blamed for not being born a hero'. It is unfair to blame Abbey for his narrowness; and his strictness, however much it hampered and vexed John, ensured Fanny's reaching hale and hearty old age. Abbey's worst act of omission was what appears now to be his callousness over the death of Tom, but it is likely enough that he was genuinely apprehensive of infection: John had had to undergo it, but why should Fanny?

Abbey is, however, most chastised for his treatment of Keats – the world in general hardly knows of or is interested in Fanny. He is sneered at first for placing Keats as apprentice to the surgeon, Thomas Hammond, in 1811, but we have no knowledge that this was in any way an autocratic choice by Abbey, and he is reviled for his indignation when, in 1816, his young ward threw up the career of medicine. It is manifestly impossible for common sense to accept this revilement. Abbey was guardian and trustee: Keats was just licensed after five years' work. What guardian in the world then or now could justifiably agree to the wasting of this apprenticeship? Moreover, Keats was not suggesting adopting instead any recognized or even, in Abbey's eyes, reputable alternative means of earning his livelihood. He proposed to give himself up to Poetry. Imagine the attitude of any hard-headed, prosaical, serious-minded merchant! Even if that merchant had been himself favourably disposed to Poetry would he, or any guardian, have been justified in approving of his ward's project – and how many tea and coffee merchants in the City to-day – or in 1816 – are believers in, or lovers of, Poetry? Abbey, who, after all, deserved well of Mrs Jennings, who had found him generous and kind, was not; and he could justify himself in his opposition by the ill-reception accorded to Keats's first venture into publication. He is reported to have said satirically of this, 'it reminds me of the Quaker's Horse which was hard to catch and good for nothing when it was caught'. This suggests a latent humour rather than a severity. Let posterity too not forget that at this stage in his career Keats was what we should now call definitely Left-wing – and that to the City, then as now, would be an additional reason for disfavour. Keats was in with Leigh Hunt and political riff-raff of that school: and it was definitely the duty of any sober, business-minded guardian to view his predilections and ambitions with disfavour. No lover of John, Tom, or Fanny Keats can possibly like Richard Abbey, but his attitude is more than defensible; it was, in all the circumstances, almost inevitable. No one at that date – or for many years after – knew that one of his wards was a genius – nor, even if they had, could it really have materially altered the verdict of prudence that he should not burn his boats and, at the outset of his career, in his early twenties, throw up a certain career for a precarious.

Let us pass on from the many misprisions to the paradoxes. The first of the three major paradoxes concerning the name and fame of John Keats is the extent of his elevation: it has become a limitless ascent from obscurity into a realm beyond anything but uncritical adoration. Though as early as April 15, 1817, John Taylor, of Taylor and Hessey, Keats's generous and most appreciative of publishers, writing to his own father said, 'I cannot think he will fail to become a great Poet, though I agree with you in finding much fault with his Dedication', still almost fourteen years after Keats's death, on January 9, 1835, Taylor, writing to John Clare, after being left all the MS papers of Richard Woodhouse, papers containing unpublished Poems of Keats and various other matters relating to him, had to say, 'I don't know when it will be possible for me to do anything with them. I should like to reprint a complete edition of Keats's Poems, with several of his letters, but the world cares nothing for him. I fear that even 250 copies would not sell'. It was not, in fact, until 1840 that it was thought worth while to collect and publish an edition of Keats's Poems by themselves, without, that is, Poems by Shelley and Coleridge – so slow was recognition to spread beyond the personal circle of Keats's friends.

But, once begun, the spread of recognition has never ceased and its pace has accelerated immeasurably; it has not only widened to all the world so that if anyone to-day were to ask 'what are Keats?' it would be a question that would place the asker for ever in the category of the utterly illiterate, but it has passed all conceivable bounds. When, for example, in 1933, Mr M. R. Ridley paid Keats the tribute of publishing a detailed, scholarly examination into his technique in his notable *Keats' Craftsmanship*, the writer of the leading article reviewing the book in the *Times Literary Supplement* castigated him for daring to criticize, describing him 'as not altogether unscathed by the disease of superiority to Keats', and adding, 'he is more than a little lacking in humility'. Mr Middleton Murry, however, goes in much deeper: possibly by way of balance to his onslaught on the tender-hearted girl Keats had so passionately loved, he passes in his *Keats and Shakespeare* to utterly extravagant praise of Keats himself: many, perhaps, may not be disposed to disagree with Mr Murry when he states that Keats was 'one of the bravest and wisest and most beautiful spirits this

England has been privileged to engender', though that is, one would think, going to the limit of allowable praise of anyone, but when, three pages later, he writes, 'There is no man living, and no man has ever lived, who has the right to pass judgment upon Keats. It is an act of terrible presumption', one may well be puzzled as to the function of any reasoned, rational critic: to adopt this attitude is to pass wholly into the role of hyperbolic adulator. It is not an attitude that would have commended itself in the least to Keats, who was not only a great poet but also a great man – not at all necessarily the same thing. Keats, doubtless, could not be unconscious of his possession of genius, though the most he permitted himself to write as to that was the simple 'I think I shall be among the English poets after my death', but he was as nearly free from the weakness of vanity as a man can be. He held, as he wrote to B. R. Haydon on May 10, 1817, that 'there is no greater Sin after the seven than to flatter oneself into the belief of being a great Poet': and, in consequence, he continually, as he passed upward in his power, critized sternly work that he had just completed as, for example, when he wrote of *Isabella* that it 'is what I should call were I a reviewer a weak-sided Poem with an amusing sober-sadness about it': he felt it to be, in his own word, 'smokeable'. Again, in his lovely Preface to *Endymion* all he says with a modesty that ought to have disarmed any critic is, 'It is just that this youngster should die away: a sad thought for me, if I had not some hope that while it is dwindling I may be plotting and fitting myself for verses fit to live'. Keats, throughout his life – until, at any rate, the fire of consumption ate away his strength – had a clear-eyed greatness of vision which would have made him both satirical and vexed at the uncritical adulation heaped upon him. And, indeed, such is particularly unsuited to work much of which is definitely immature in the sense that, however delicate or delightful, it was work beyond which the writer rapidly passed. It is sound to say with Mr Ridley, 'the critics who are not too proud to accept Keats' self-analysis are wiser than those who, prompted by a serene vanity and a misplaced confidence in their own analytical powers, present us with a Keats in their own image'.

The second of the great paradoxes concerning Keats is that it is in the twentieth century that his elevation has been so tremendously heightened; and yet nothing is more clear than that his spirit is alien to that of to-day. Moreover, it is amongst Americans, from Miss Amy Lowell down to Mr Holland Day, that he has found some of his most attentive admirers, and the spirit of modern America is not precisely that of one who 'loved the principle of Beauty in all things': indeed in October, 1818, Keats expressed the view that 'the humanity of the United States can never reach the sublime'.

The age is an age of iconoclasm, of destruction, of fierceness of competition where the machine made by Man to be his servant has widely become his master, of industrialism and urban crowdings – with such an age it is difficult to imagine Keats as in the least degree in sympathy, Keats as he was, as he exists for us in his Poems and his Letters: that he would have been different had he been with us now is, of course, obvious, even without the specific indications of growth and oncoming change that are to be found in his writings and to which attention must be called in due course. But these are beside the point, which is that, essentially opposed as he is to so much that is to-day regarded as of supreme importance, he is still taken into the heart of the world as almost no other writer has ever been or is likely ever again to be.

This is all the more strange when it is considered that not only his spirit and his thought but also the actual prosody of his Poetry is wholly diverse from the fashion of the world that has so acclaimed him as its own. Keats never allowed himself the indulgence of free verse, he never wrote according to unfettered fancy without form or rhythm. On the contrary, he gave himself up to strictly 'disciplined verse' (to use the phrase employed in 1948 to describe, unattractively, a certain writer's orderly technique); he confined his Poetry – apart from humorous verse for his little sister or friends – to such measures as the staid formality of the Spenserian stanza, to rhymed couplets, to regular blank verse, to formalized metres, and – worst of all – to the severe limitations of the sonnet, despised and even detested by the modernists. The paradox of his world-crown is indeed a strange one.

The reason for it is, presumably, the existence in his life of a quality not as a general rule inherent in the lives of those whose eminence is due to their writings, namely, drama. Shelley had drama of a much more spectacular kind, both in his relations with Harriet and with Mary and also in the hour of his death; and he too died young and with 'unfulfilled renown'. But there is, with Shelley, no comparable sense as of a Greek tragedy as broods inexorably over Keats, no deepening down, down of the shadows till the pathos is extreme, till a writer in the *Times Literary Supplement* is so clearly justified in calling the last year of Keats's life 'perhaps the most purely painful extant record of human suffering'.

That by itself would not suffice to account for the intense

and the universal interest in, and acclaim of, Keats. To this must be added the great truth of Keats's personal attraction. Shelley was immensely attractive too, but he was never as simply and humanly lovable as Keats. Whether or no Keats's spirit was 'brave and wise', it was unquestionably 'beautiful' – even as he himself was beautiful – not 'a pard-like spirit' as Shelley was to describe himself after Keats's death, but a spirit of lambency and light.

Before consumption ravaged him, mind, body and soul, he must have been a delight to look upon, very short of stature as he was, with his abnormally bright and intelligent hazel eyes (which, according to Joseph Severn, 'seemed almost to throw a light before his face'), his lovely, golden-brown hair, his most shapely profile, and his sensitive mouth: above all, his expression, 'sweet and mild', to use the description written by Fanny Keats in 1881 or 'sweet and intellectual' in 1884. He was as personally beloved by those who knew him during his life as he has since become to those who can only read him or read about him. The old idea, long, long held, was that he was a sensuous weakling, 'snuffed out', in Byron's characteristically satirical phrase, 'by an article', the bitter polemics of the *Quarterly Review* and *Blackwood's Magazine*. That idea is dead, at least amongst all who know anything of him at all. So far from being namby-pamby, he was the exact converse: he was a lad of pugnacity, definitely enjoying fisticuffs. Moreover, he was extremely intelligent, tender-hearted, whimsical and merrily full of quips: no more delightful or more interesting companion can ever have been. In addition, he was modest and – a fact which so many forget or ignore – he was natural, both to a degree singularly seldom true of poets.

Take, for example, this courageous, humorous philosophy,

written to his friend, John Hamilton Reynolds in 1817, anxious as Keats was at that period over the health of his dearly loved brother, Tom: 'why don't you,' asked Keats, 'as I do, look unconcernedly at what may be called more particularly Heart-vexations? They never surprize me – lord! a man should have the fine point of his soul taken off to become fit for this world.'

Add – almost in parenthesis – that over and above his poetic genius he was as attractive a letter-writer as any England has ever produced; and finally, that, beyond all these attributes and gifts, he had as another of his friends, Benjamin Bailey, could write as long after his death as 1849, 'a soul of utter integrity'. No wonder, then, that the intensity and poignancy of his apparent failure should have sunk so profoundly into the heart of Mankind. But the second of the strange paradoxes remains, nonetheless.

The third paradox – possibly the strangest of the three – is that though the whole of the literate world knows of him, yet it would be very difficult to find any, outside the small band of Professors of Literature or those at school or college who have a specific, academic purpose in studying him, who have read more than a very small fraction of his work. This in so unpoetic an age is probably true of almost all poets, but in the case of Keats it is most marked in both the diametrically opposed directions. His status is higher than that of almost any writer who has ever lived: the facts concerning his life are established to a degree of completeness and intimacy which is more than is the case in the lives of all but a handful: of the possibilities of studying a great poet in his workshop, 'comparable opportunities are,' as Professor H. W. Garrod has said, 'hardly to be found elsewhere' – and the extent of the work by which he is known to the mass of mankind is, at most, only a few hundred lines. Hardly one in ten thousand who would be quite indignant if accused of not having read Keats has read *Endymion*, his longest work, much fewer have read both *Endymion* and *Lamia* – and almost no one has read his one completed play, *Otho the Great* – dismissed, as a rule, even by his closest adherers, as mere hack-work because it was written in collaboration with Charles Brown, to Brown's scenario. One could go further still: *The Fall of Hyperion* is known to specialist students; it is not read by the world which speaks of its knowledge of *Hyperion*, but probably – if examined – would have to admit to acquaintance only with the opening 21 lines – just as the world is as familiar with the first line of *Endymion* as it is unmindful of the remaining 4150. And yet there are those who attach as much importance to *The Fall of Hyperion* as to anything Keats wrote: Mr Murry even calls it 'the profoundest and most sublime of his poems'.

These vicissitudes, misprisions, paradoxes and surprises are worth thought. There is now no longer room or need for a fresh recapitulation of the facts of the life of Keats. These are set out, fully and finally, in Dorothy Hewlett's *Adonais*, published in 1937. She had before her, first of all, the foundations laid by Lord Houghton (then Richard Monckton Milnes) in 1848, then the building carefully, studiously erected by Sir Sidney Colvin in 1918, and, thirdly, the additions gathered with great industry and set out with not a little prolixity by Miss Amy Lowell in 1925.

Miss Hewlett's purpose was a biographical survey of Keats's life rather than a critical examination of his writings; this latter she hardly attempted, contenting herself in the main with collecting and setting down the opinions of others as to the Poems. It is not therefore the purpose of this new study to dwell yet again upon the biographical facts except in so far as they affect the understanding and appreciation of the Poems, some at least of which will be read and loved as long as beauty of thought and expression in the English tongue survive upon the earth as part of Man's inheritance. Often, beyond doubt, the facts do so affect understanding and appreciation, so much so that it is seriously fallacious to speak of any study of Keats the man as distinct from Keats the poet. The two are one to as intense a degree as can be said of any one, and to dissever them is quite impossible. Keats, it must always be remembered, is in many ways – though not always in ways in which he is portrayed – one of the most personal of poets. But the facts of his life are now so well known – or at least they can be: they are accessible in their completeness to any and every reader who desires to become acquainted with them. And repetition is tedious, the last thing that Keats ever is or that any one writing about him and his work should be. It is fitting, therefore, rather to assume now a reasonable degree of acquaintance with the main course of the moving mystery of his life, remembering always his own prophetic words written to Miss Jeffrey, of Teignmouth, on June 9, 1819, 'one of the great reasons that the English have produced the finest writers in the world is that the English world has ill-treated them during their lives and foster'd them after their deaths'.

II

SUNRISE

ON JULY 25, 1816 – that is three months and six days before he attained the age of twenty-one* – John Keats received his certificate licensing him to practise as an Apothecary, and ceased from that moment forward to take interest in the profession of medicine to so complete a degree that it is probable that the vast majority of those who read any of his writings are wholly unfamiliar with the fact that he was ever in any way associated with it. It is true that at a late stage in his life he contemplated endeavouring to secure a post as ship's surgeon, in part as a means of earning much-needed money and in part to restore his health, but it remained a contemplation only and was soon abandoned even as that.

In 1816 he had been undergoing medical training for five years, almost a fifth, that is, of the total number that were to be his, but after becoming licensed there are only three references to this long professional experience, one in a letter, one in speech, and one in the whole of his poetry. The first of the former is contained in sentences written in his famous journal-letter of September, 1819, to George and Georgiana Keats, 'I dare say you have altered also – every man does – our bodies every seven years are completely fresh-material'd – seven years ago it was not this hand that clench'd itself against Hammond'. Mr Maurice Buxton

---

*Unless indeed, as Professor H. W. Garrod has suggested, he was born, not in October, 1795, but in June, the certificate being marked 'of full age'.

JOHN KEATS: THE PRINCIPLE OF BEAUTY

Forman says that this phrase 'points to a serious rupture as the cause of his quitting his apprenticeship to Hammond', but that is the kind of guess-work from which Keats has so often suffered: there is no evidence for its truth; when he entered Guy's Hospital in October, 1815, he had with him, as was necessary, Hammond's certificate of good behaviour. It seems more probable that it points to nothing more serious than a reference to one of the quick surges of pugnacity characteristic of Keats's boyhood, 'a wisp of straw conflagration' as it was called.

The second reference, in speech, is the poignant, indeed terrible, beginning of the end when Keats had his serious hæmorrhage at Wentworth Place on the night of February 3, 1820, and, looking at the drop of blood he had coughed up, is stated to have said quietly to Charles Brown, 'I know the colour of that blood. It's arterial blood. I cannot be deceived in that colour. That drop of blood is my death warrant. I must die'. The actual words read a little as though they were rather a dramatic recollection, but the medical testimony is unchallenged.

The third reference, the first in point of time, the only one in Keats's poetry, occurs in the fourth book of *Endymion*, line 1667, where he writes, '*And warm with dew at ooze from living blood*', where it is the more singular as it does not seem to be at all appropriate.

The absence of all other allusions is unexpected since medicine abounds in striking illustrations: it strengthens the natural belief that with whatever mind Keats entered upon it, he came to view it at best with indifference, at worst with repugnance. There is nothing on record to support a supposition that he was forced into his medical training: it is more probable that as a boy of sixteen he accepted it – no doubt at his guardian's suggestion or even direction – as a suitable profession and then passed mentally beyond, or at any rate, away from it. Certain it is that as soon as licensed he gave it up for ever. By July, 1816, he was busy with what concerned him and in his case has concerned Mankind, much more, namely, the pursuit of Poetry. From that he never deviated. 'I find,' he wrote to his friend, John Hamilton Reynolds, from Carisbrooke on April 17, 1817, 'that I cannot exist without poetry – without eternal poetry – half the day will not do – the whole of it.'

He has left us scattered through his letters, in which he discussed with his intimates so much and so profoundly, a number of sayings about this pursuit of Poetry. Of these the best known is the third of the three axioms written to his publisher, John Taylor, from Hampstead on February 27, 1818, 'That if Poetry comes not as naturally as the leaves to a tree it had better not come at all'. This does not sound a difficult saying: on the contrary, it sounds simple, indeed convincing: but it has not been so regarded by all; in fact, it has even been suggested that a whole book could be written upon its real meaning. Certainly a whole book – many whole books – could be written upon the writing of Poetry, in the course of which Keats's axiom would be fully discussed. But in itself the axiom is completely straightforward and there is little doubt but that Keats, who had, as his letters continually show, a delicious sense of humour, would be much amused at the trouble of its correct interpretation. All writers – if they become sufficiently famous to attract attention – in particular, all poets, have upon their backs the burden of the cleverness of commentators who seek to extract from their words some meaning hidden from lesser intelligences. And this is particularly true of

JOHN KEATS: THE PRINCIPLE OF BEAUTY

poets whose craft is as a general rule so great a mystery to all who have never wrestled with it.

In his poetry Keats indulged in imaginative flights of fancy, inevitably and fittingly: but in his letters this – again inevitably and fittingly – is not so. Why should it be? A man writing to his friends writes what he wants to tell them, what they want to know: he may be sportive, whimsical, or ironic, but he writes to be understood. Is it really too much to ask in the name of common sense – so often omitted in these discussions – that Keats should be taken in this most interesting and thoughtful letter to his publisher to mean exactly what he says?

The difficulty, doubtless, is the mystery of Poetry, the whole power of production of which is often so completely misunderstood. The most complete example of the opaqueness of the mists of ignorance which ever came my way was when, some years ago, it fell to my lot to preside over a gathering of young writers. In the course of the discussion a lady rose to make some remarks about the supreme virtue of inspiration and to clinch her argument she instanced the two *Hyperions*: in her view *Hyperion* was immeasurably superior to *The Fall of Hyperion* – the opinion generally held, which it will be necessary for me to examine later in this book. It was obvious from her remarks that she was under the impression that Keats sat down and wrote *Hyperion* straight out without correction or pause for reflection and then, when inspiration had ceased, turned forthwith to the secondary process of emendation and revision resulting in *The Fall of Hyperion*. Abysmal incomprehension of the poet's art could hardly go further; and – which was really significant – no one of the company, even though all were by way of being literary folk, found the illustration in any way singular or absurd. And indeed it is usual to find that people in general suppose that Poetry comes to those who have it in them to produce it at all much as one turns on the bath-tap – and that that is right, that is what Keats's sentence meant.

Yet nothing can be more certain than that Keats did not mean that. I do not think that anyone who has ever written, or ever, let us say, seriously tried to write, Poetry would question the view that what Keats meant was that Poetry had better not be forced, but rather should be written by its creator when in the mood, by one who feels the tide of inspiration within and yields thought and sensitiveness to it. The axiom he was enunciating is the same as that he expressed in his hardly known *Fairy's Song*, where he writes,

> 'For I was taught in Paradise
> To ease my heart of melodies.'

Poetry, if Keats's axiom be accepted, should not be written as a task, mood or no mood, as, for instance, Robert Browning at one stage in his life, setting himself down resolutely every morning from ten to one, tried to compel his mind to write it – with unsatisfying results. And this axiom is not upset by Keats's own practice in the Isle of Wight and at Oxford on *Endymion* when he set himself to write fifty lines a day: that was at a time when he had wholly devoted his powers to the poem, when he was, definitely, in the mood, when, as he writes at the beginning of Book I,

> 'tis with full happiness that I
> Will trace the story of Endymion.
> The very music of the name has gone
> Into my being, and each pleasant scene

JOHN KEATS: THE PRINCIPLE OF BEAUTY

*Is growing fresh before me as the green
Of our own vallies: so I will begin
Now while I cannot hear the city's din.*

Keats did not write remarks about Poetry without expressing his deepest convictions, and to his convictions he unswervingly adhered. Poetry was his goddess and he served her with all his being, writing when inspiration was on him, studying when it was not – until, at least, he came to the penultimate phase of his life when the shadows were closing so remorselessly in on his youth.

There are many inexplicable, or at least unexplained, things about him – as, indeed, about all men of genius. One of the first of these is the absence of beginnings. All young folk, who write at all, write from childhood. In his case, when the brevity of his writing life is considered and the phenomenal speed at which he passed to greatness, it might be expected that this would be especially true, that there would be an abundance of juvenilia. But Keats seems to have been the exception in every way. He did not begin to be studious till he was fifteen: then he plunged with exceptional absorption – not into writing but into reading. It may be that he wrote and destroyed what he wrote: we know that he had the carelessness of the very great and that but for the indefatigable admiration, zeal, and industry of friends like Richard Woodhouse and Brown many of his MSS – scribbled down and tossed aside – would have been lost. But in any case he sprang into Poetry like Minerva – not full-born in the sense that no growth was possible, far from it, but with a degree of ease and mastery that is only little acclaimed because it took him so short a space of time before he had outsoared it.

SUNRISE

His early work is not at all impeccable – as no one realized more clearly than he himself; and if that had been all that he had had to offer to the world it would not have been revived or remembered by anybody. It has abundance of the faults of youth, immaturity of thought, lapses of taste, precosity, over-elaboration, and so forth; but even from the first there is for the discerning – made easy for all by the after-knowledge – an opulence as well as a freshness and a simplicity which in their combination are throughout the peculiar characteristic of the Poetry of Keats.

There is doubt as to which is the earliest of his poems that we possess. It would be appropriate if Lord Houghton is right in placing as early as 1812 the *Imitation from Spenser*, with its opening lines,

> *Now Morning from her orient chamber came,*
> *And her first footsteps touch'd a verdant hill;*

but it seems probable that that is several years later and that the boy's first footsteps touch the verdant hill of Poetry in the following sonnet, written, so Keats told Woodhouse in 1819, a few days after the death of his grandmother, Mrs Jennings, in December, 1814, but not disclosed (until 1819 when Keats told Woodhouse he had never told anyone, not even his brothers, of it) or ever published until so late as 1876:

> *As from the darkening gloom a silver dove*
> *Upsoars, and darts into the Eastern light,*
> *On pinions that naught moves but pure delight,*
> *So fled thy soul into the realms above,*
> *Regions of peace and everlasting love;*

JOHN KEATS: THE PRINCIPLE OF BEAUTY

Where happy spirits, crown'd with circlets bright
Of starry beam, and gloriously bedight,
Taste the high joy none but the blest can prove.
There thou or joinest the immortal quire
In melodies that even Heaven fair
Fill with superior bliss, or, at Desire
Of the omnipotent Father, cleavest the air
On holy message sent — What pleasure's higher?
Wherefore does any grief our joy impair?

This is of particular interest not only because it is one of the very earliest — if not actually the earliest — of Keats's poems, but because it is, in every respect, characteristic. It is not first-class — obviously — but it has nevertheless, to my ear and mind at least, a singular charm: it is pure Keats, however young, and could have come from no other mint. But there is another, and a stronger, reason for setting it down: it is a sonnet in the Petrarchan form, the most difficult because the most closely knit and regulated of all poetic forms. The sonnet is to-day, as I have already said, despised and even detested by the modernists — in spite of Wordsworth's adjuration not to scorn it. Yet the sonnet is a form that innumerable pens have attempted, and though there are, admittedly, occasional fine ones by various creators, only four in English can be said ever really to have mastered it: they are Shakespeare (who, incidentally, chose his own form, a considerably easier one, technically, than the Petrarchan), Milton, Wordsworth, and Keats. It became Keats's favourite form for short poems, and some of his are securely lodged among the great inheritances of literature. Here, early in his twentieth year, he writes his first, a private, personal tribute to the grandmother he loved.

SUNRISE

It may be fitting here to record the first of my own two small personal experiences in direct connexion with Keats since it concerns the two sonnets printed by Professor Garrod immediately before the one quoted above in his definitive edition of Keats's Poems, published in 1939. He says there that they were first printed in the *Times Literary Supplement* of May 21, 1914 – the one mistake in his great work: they were first printed in *The Times* itself, together with a long article explaining their history and their place in Keats's youth. I know that, as I first identified them as authentic – with the expert assistance of Sir Sidney Colvin, most courteously given – and wrote the explanatory article. At that date I was at work in Printing House Square and was, during Sir Bruce Richmond's absence, acting literary editor: a copy of Keats's first volume, the *Poems* 1817, was brought to me with the two sonnets written in on a blank page in Keats's beautiful handwriting; it was the copy Keats had given John Hamilton Reynolds. I well remember the thrill of handling the little volume and seeing the Sonnets, and Sir Sydney Colvin, to whom I at once took them, old as he was, was equally thrilled. Both sonnets were written at one of the occasions when Keats, visiting Leigh Hunt, indulged not only in the exercise of competitive sonnet-writing but also in the harmless conceit described: another occasion is known when two gentlemen and not three ladies came in during the 'coronation'. Keats wrote his *Ode to Apollo* by way of apology for poetic presumption, and the whole episode and the productions consequent upon it have the spontaneity, the lack of pomp and pretentiousness so characteristic of Keats who, it is said, boy-like, refused to remove his chaplet for any visitor.

JOHN KEATS: THE PRINCIPLE OF BEAUTY

ON RECEIVING A LAUREL CROWN FROM
LEIGH HUNT

Minutes are flying swiftly, and as yet
Nothing unearthly has enticed my brain
Into a delphic labyrinth — I would fain
Catch an unmortal thought to pay the debt
I owe to the kind Poet who has set
Upon my ambitious head a glorious gain.
Two bending laurel sprigs — 'tis nearly pain
To be conscious of such a Coronet.
Still time is fleeting, and no dream arises
Gorgeous as I would have it — only I see
A trampling down of what the world most prizes
Turbans and crowns and blank regality;
And then I run into most wild surmises
Of all the many glories that may be.

TO THE LADIES WHO SAW ME CROWN'D

What is there in the universal Earth
More lovely than a wreath from the bay tree?
Haply a Halo round the moon — a glee
Circling from three sweet pair of lips in mirth;
And haply you will say the dewy birth
Of morning Roses — riplings tenderly
Spread by the Halcyon's breast upon the sea —
But these comparisons are nothing worth —
Then is there nothing in the world so fair?
The silvery tears of April? — Youth of May?
Or June that breathes out life for butterflies?
No — none of these can from my favourite bear
Away the Palm — yet shall it ever pay
Due reverence to your most sovereign eyes.

SUNRISE

The Times, in May, 1914, had just been reduced in price to one penny and a big newspaper rivalry was on: it may well be that it was because of that I was given so much space in which to enlarge upon Keats. *Punch*, I remember, was sarcastic – which grieved me as I had only sought enthusiastically to honour the Poet I loved. But still, these many years after, I continue unashamedly to think that, though the two sonnets may not deserve to be termed great, they are rich with the promise of greatness, quite unmistakeably from the mind of Keats: who but he could ever have written that description of June? And, as Sir Sydney Colvin at once pointed out to me, the conclusion of the first of these two sonnets is rather closely a forerunner of the beginning of Book III of *Endymion*, with its question in line 22,

Are then regalities all gilded masks?

That is entirely true, always, of Keats: his work varies in merit, inevitably and considerably, but it is all of a piece, perpetually reminiscent of thought and invariably possessing a quality peculiarly his own. Mr Middleton Murry has said, and with the approval of Mr Maurice Buxton Forman, that 'those who cannot understand Keats's love, will never understand his poetry, for these two things spring from a single source'. Two very eminent authorities indeed; but let us not forget that Mr Murry dislikes Fanny Brawne so intensely as to be incapable of understanding Keats's love and, moreover, that Keats had already devoted his whole being to Poetry – for example, he had declared, as early as April 18, 1817, 'I find I cannot exist without poetry – without eternal poetry' – and also he had written a very considerable proportion of his total output before he had ever heard of Fanny Brawne's existence. This latter fact would, perhaps, not invalidate the statement if, on falling in love, Keats's Poetry had undergone a marked change in character – but it did not. He grew, and grew immeasurably; but he did not change. His early Poetry bears the same relation to his later as apple-blossom bears to apple: the one is the outcome in maturity of the other. And the astonishing, almost exotic rapidity and magnitude of Keats's maturity does not alter the truth that throughout his life his work was in essence all of a piece. Through it, from first to last, run certain veins of richest ore, 'the principle of Beauty (or, as he has it also 'the mighty abstract Idea of Beauty') in all things' most conspicuously, and continually associated with it a chivalrous devotion and a tenderness not so much for women or any one woman as for Womanhood. There are, to supplement and emphasize this, the memorable sentences in two of his letters to his friend, Benjamin Bailey; in the first, written on January 23, 1818, after the reference to Bailey's saying 'Why should Woman suffer?' 'These things are, and he who feels how incompetent the most skyey Knight errantry is to heal this bruised fairness is like a sensitive leaf on the hot hand of thought'. The second, written on June 10, 1818, is 'I would reject a petrarchal coronation – on account of my dying day, and because women have Cancers'. Who else but Keats would reason so? 'For Spenser,' Professor Dowden wrote years ago, 'behind each woman made to worship or love rises a sacred presence – Womanhood itself.' Towards that elevation Keats steadily moved throughout his life.

It is with the knowledge of this mind in Keats that we can now read the three sonnets on the subject of woman the first of which begins,

SUNRISE

> *Woman! when I behold thee flippant, vain*

with its passionate cry in the third,

> *God! she is like a milk-white lamb that bleats*
> *For man's protection,*

the chivalrous tenderness of which is almost as out of fashion in 1948 as the dependence of girls who manned – or rather womanned – gun-sites in their 'teens.

Sonnets – many sonnets: there are no fewer than twenty-one in the thirty-three poems contained in Keats's first published volume; that alone would put it out of court, unrecognized, unpraised, if newly issued to-day.

And so to 1817, medical circles exchanged for literary, prescriptions for poems, the year of Keats's friendship with Leigh Hunt, the popular (and unpopular) writer, politician and editor, and B. R. Haydon, the vain-glorious, egotistical painter, with, too, a widening band of interesting and ardent young men, the year of 'the immortal dinner' at Haydon's when Keats met Wordsworth and Lamb 'got exceedingly merry and exquisitely witty', the year of the writing of *Endymion*, the year of the publication of the first volume.

Most of the slender contents of this are well known to, and loved by, all real adherents of Keats, but they are as little read – all but one – by the world now as they were at the time of their publication. And this, though it may pain the small company of the faithful, is not surprising. Most of the poems are purely personal and some of them are very young indeed. It can hardly be open to doubt what their fate would be if submitted to-day by an unknown boy to any publisher: he might like them, he might even see in them poetic promise for the future, but he would certainly reject them – unless the author was prepared to pay for their publication. They would not be a commercial proposition to-day, and they were not in 1817 when the market for Poetry was so much more profitable that it was not at all unreasonable for Keats – or for any other young writer of ambition, industry, and attainments – to hope to make a living by its sale.

It would hardly have made any difference, but Keats did not include among the sonnets two that had appeared on March 9, 1817 in *The Examiner* and *The Champion* – they were obviously too late: his volume was published on March 3, and he was clearly holding these two back for magazine publication: but the first is among his finest and both deal with a subject then much before the British public. The second, beginning

> *Haydon! forgive me that I cannot speak*
> *Definitively on these mighty things,*

is personal and introductory to the first which is called simply,

ON SEEING THE ELGIN MARBLES

> *My spirit is too weak – mortality*
> *Weighs heavily on me like unwilling sleep,*
> *And each imagin'd pinnacle and steep*
> *Of godlike hardship tells me I must die*
> *Like a sick Eagle looking at the sky.*
> *Yet 'tis a gentle luxury to weep*
> *That I have not the cloudy winds to keep*
> *Fresh for the opening of the morning's eye.*
> *Such dim-conceived glories of the brain*

SUNRISE

Bring round the heart an undescribable feud;
So do these wonders a most dizzy pain,
That mingles Grecian grandeur with the rude
Wasting of old time – with a billowy main –
A sun – a shadow of a magnitude.

There is nothing immature about that: it is a sonnet none but a great poet could have written – and it is omitted from the volume which contains much that is remembered only for the author's later glories. *Imitation of Spenser, Specimen of an Induction to a Poem, Calidore,* a fragment, personal verses *To Some Ladies, Epistles* to his brother and to two friends, also a number of personal sonnets to his brothers, to Haydon and his friends – not one of these would have in itself lasting value. And yet in most there are touches of pure Poetry, felicities peculiarly characteristic of Keats repaying thought and study. Maybe it is invidious to single any out, but they are at least testimonies to truth – and any reader can make his or her own selection. Thus Keats notes the swan that *sparkled his jetty eyes'*: he asks of a Poet rambling in the evening,

Would he naught see but the dark, silent blue
With all its diamonds trembling through?

and writes of a second ramble

in the happy fields
What time the sky-lark shakes the tremulous dew
From his lush clover covert,

and of a third,

returning home at evening,
He mourns that day so soon has glided by;

JOHN KEATS: THE PRINCIPLE OF BEAUTY

> *E'en like the passage of an angel's tear*
> *That falls through the clear ether silently;*

just as he had asked in his first published poem *O Solitude!* printed in *The Examiner* of May 5, 1816, by Leigh Hunt and initialled simply J. K.,

> *Let me my vigils keep*
> *'Mongst boughs pavilion'd, where the deer's swift leap*
> *Startles the wild bee from the fox-glove bell.*

Herein already, at the very outset of his literary life, is that richness of detail, that felicity of description so specially his. And how he loved flowers! His Poetry from first to last is full of them and we know how poignantly he wrote to his friend, James Rice, on February 16, 1820, 'I muse with the greatest affection on every flower I have known from my infancy – their shapes and colours are as new to me as if I had just created them with a superhuman fancy'. This was the Poet who in a little known sonnet of 1818 speaks of *'that queen of secrecy, the violet'*, and begins the first Poem in his first book (after the dedication to Leigh Hunt in which also he writes of *'baskets bringing ears of corn, Roses, and pinks, and violets'*), with the fresh young enchantment of the lines,

> *I stood tiptoe upon a little hill,*
> *The air was cooling, and so very still,*
> *That the sweet buds which with a modest pride*
> *Pull droopingly, in slanting curve aside,*
> *Their scantly leaved, and finely tapering stems*
> *Had not yet lost those starry diadems*
> *Caught from the early sobbing of the morn.*

SUNRISE

and, a little later, the well-known

> *Here are sweet peas, on tiptoe for a flight;*
> *With wings of gentle flush o'er delicate white,*
> *And taper fingers catching at all things,*
> *To bind them all about with tiny rings.*

It is all so young, so disingenuous, and so charming – as well as all so exactly observed and recorded that it might well have disarmed hostile criticism, but, for reasons political rather than poetic, that was not to be: the dedication to Leigh Hunt was unquestionably an error in literary tactics.

The volume ends with *Sleep and Poetry* which begins in vein similar to the lines just quoted, with the questions,

> *What is more gentle than a wind in summer?*
> *What is more soothing than the pretty hummer*
> *That stays one moment in an open flower,*
> *And buzzes cheerily from bower to bower?*
> *What is more tranquil than a musk-rose blowing*
> *In a green island, far from all men's knowing?*
> *More healthful than the leafiness of dales?*
> *More secret than a nest of nightingales?*
> *More serene than Cordelia's countenance?*
> *More full of visions than a high romance?*
> *What, but thee, Sleep?*

All Keats in these lines, and yet a Keats in bud rather than in blossom. He was very fond of this kind of imaginative reiteration: it occurs again, ninety lines on, in

> *Life is the rose's hope while yet unblown;*
> *The reading of an ever-changing tale;*
> *The light uplifting of a maiden's veil;*

JOHN KEATS: THE PRINCIPLE OF BEAUTY

A pigeon tumbling in clear summer air;
A laughing school-boy, without grief or care,
Riding the springy branches of an elm.

The poem has more to it than these delicate, delightful descriptions: it has thought and futurity, and there will be need to refer to these later. Here it will suffice to say that it – and the volume – achieved no success. It received many more reviews than a comparable volume would to-day, some sarcastic, some hostile, but several friendly; but it did not sell; indeed C. and J. Ollier, the publishers, received a number of caustic complaints, one from 'a gentleman who told us,' they wrote to George Keats, 'he considered it "no better than a take in".' To-day the world has concluded that it contains one famous sonnet, so famous that it need not be here quoted, that *On first looking into Chapman's Homer*. It is a little difficult to understand the universality of the fame of this: it has greatness undeniably, 'a pure serene', in fact (though those words were a later emendation) and its conclusion,

Silent, upon a peak in Darien,

is masterly; but it does not seem – to me, at least – to merit selection above all others of Keats, save, perhaps, *Bright Star*. Those two are in everyone's knowledge; the rest are not, and the one just quoted on the Elgin Marbles most certainly deserves equal fame. However, that is the way of the world, and in this case it has the support of the eminent, Professor Garrod saying that at 8 Dean Street (now Stainer Street) Keats 'did his first great deed in poetry', namely, the writing of this sonnet, though earlier in the introduction to his edition of Keats's Poems, he speaks of him as 'a poet for the first time decisive' in respect of the volume of 1820 – which seems the more accurate view.

All this first volume is really preparatory, even though it is only just to add that never before in literary history has preparation been in itself so felicitous. And the same can be said – was said by Keats himself without the addition of praise – of his second volume, *Endymion*: 'it must rather,' he wrote in the first draft of his preface, 'be considered as an endeavour than a thing accomplish'd.' All the good he expected from it, so he wrote to Haydon, was the fruit of experience he hoped to gather in his next Poem.

Endymion, his longest Poem, is to-day read by few, even by very few: in itself it is in no way the foundation for his fame and this though, as far back as October 8, 1817, he had written to Bailey the celebrated sentence, 'a long Poem is a test of invention which I take to be the Polar Star of Poetry, as Fancy is the Sails, and Imagination the Rudder'. And the reason is not far to seek, especially in an age which will not give to Poetry the attention necessary for the appreciation of long pieces. Keats does not overcome the test, in that, though he is full of invention, it is invention of detail and not invention of plot. Plots, throughout his life, were his weakest point as will be further apparent: and he is conscious of the difficulty. A little earlier in this same letter to Bailey he wrote of the test that he had set himself, adding, 'I must make 4000 lines of one bare circumstance and fill them with Poetry'. This is not so much a challenge as a confession and it leaves unanswered the question, why decide beforehand on the number, 4000? Having so decided, he had to elaborate on the 'one bare circumstance' ('Peace, ho! the moon sleeps with Endymion') which is all that ancient mythology supplies and, though he was successful, even brilliantly so, in 'filling it with Poetry', he could not – or did not – make a consecutive, or even intelligible, story. As Professor Francis T. Palgrave wrote in the notes to his beautiful edition of Poems, published in 1885, 'Splendid as are the foliage and the flowers, Endymion is an almost pathless intricacy of story: a Paradise without a plan.'

Keats himself never thought highly of his poem: with that clear-sighted, self-criticism which is so characteristic of his intelligent modesty, he makes a number of deprecatory references to it. He calls it 'the slipshod *Endymion*', and as there is nothing whatever in the verse that is deserving of such a description, it is obvious that he is referring to the structure; and in his letter of August, 1820, to Shelley, thanking for Shelley's invitation to him to stay with him in Italy, acknowledging the *Cenci* and giving him the famous advice, 'curb your magnanimity, and be more of an artist, and load every rift of your subject with ore', he adds, 'is not this extraordinary talk from the writer of Endymion, whose mind was like a pack of scattered cards?'

And yet what cards! *Endymion* is not to be read through as a story but enjoyed in small sections for its copious felicity. There have been those who have sought to clarify it, to see in it a rich allegory, to identify the moon with Poetry and the Indian maid with human love, the two blending into one; but their success is dubious and as they seldom agree they can well be left, untroubled, to their divergences. But read for its detail, for its lovely descriptions, read as a young poet's dream, his forging of the tools of his genius, trying his wings that he might attempt mightier flights – the view he himself took of its production – *Endymion* is a justification of that first line which is so universally known.

SUNRISE

Indeed, the whole of its opening has a delicate fragrance and freshness for which there is little parallel:

A thing of beauty is a joy for ever:
Its loveliness increases; it will never
Pass into nothingness; but still will keep
A bower quiet for us, and a sleep
Full of sweet dreams, and health, and quiet breathing.
Therefore, on every morrow, are we wreathing
A flowery band to bind us to the earth,
Spite of despondence, of the inhuman dearth
Of noble natures, of the gloomy days,
Of all the unhealthy and o'er-darkened ways
Made for our searching: yes, in spite of all,
Some shape of beauty moves away the pall
From our dark spirits. Such the sun, the moon,
Trees old, and young sprouting a shady boon
For simple sheep; and such are daffodils
With the green world they live in; and clear rills
That for themselves a cooling covert make
'Gainst the hot season: the mid-forest brake,
Rich with a sprinkling of fair musk-rose blooms:
And such too is the grandeur of the dooms
We have imagined for the mighty dead;
All lovely tales that we have heard or read:
An endless fountain of immortal drink,
Pouring into us from the heaven's brink.

   Nor do we merely feel these essences
For one short hour; no, even as the trees
That whisper round a temple become soon
Dear as the temple's self, so does the moon,
The passion poesy, glories infinite,

JOHN KEATS: THE PRINCIPLE OF BEAUTY

> *Haunt us till they become a cheering light*
> *Unto our souls, and bound to us so fast,*
> *That, whether there be shine, or gloom o'ercast,*
> *They always must be with us, or we die.*

No reader of English Poetry could for an instant mistake the authorship of those lines: every fold of the technique, every turn of the thought belongs to Keats, and Keats alone.

The first book is straightforward enough and abounding in similar felicities from

> *The surgy murmurs of the lonely sea*

to

> *The Morphean fount*
> *Of that fine element that visions, dreams,*
> *And fitful whims of sleep are made of, streams*
> *Into its airy channels with so subtle,*
> *So thin a breathing, not the spider's shuttle,*
> *Circled a million times within the space*
> *Of a swallow's nest-door, could delay a trace,*
> *A tinting of its quality.*

In Book I comes the chorus to Pan, which was read at Haydon's to Wordsworth: his verdict, eagerly waited on, was the cold comment, 'a very pretty piece of Paganism' – but then Wordsworth did not favour Poetry other than his own and left Keats's 1817 volume uncut.

In the second book the thread of the story begins to wander, and at one point Endymion is described as fleeing

> *Into the fearful deep, to hide his head*
> *From the clear moon, the trees and coming madness,*

SUNRISE

which seems to be entirely destructive of his whole represented pursuit. But the individual beauties persist, as, for example,

> *The cloudy rack slow journeying in the west,*
> *Like herded elephants,*

and so to the conclusion, beautiful, however strange,

> *The visions of the earth were gone and fled –*
> *He saw the giant sea above his head.*

There is little need to follow Endymion further: he is there, in two further books, each of the predecided length, for all who care to read. The political beginning of the third book is the least good of the Poem, but it soon regains its translucent freshness. The vision beneath the sea, lines 121–138 has been compared to the visions in *Richard III* and in *Prometheus Unbound*, but for my own part I care much less for the old man, his hoary head, and 'the wilder'd stranger' than for the sudden, almost inexplicable enchantment of

> *Cold – O cold indeed*
> *Were her fair limbs, and like a common weed*
> *The sea-swell took her hair.*

That is pure magic – but everyone who listens to the music of words can make his own selection.

In Book IV comes the 'roundelay' to Sorrow, with its foretaste – and such are frequent in Keats, whose work is, as has been said, all of a piece – of the *Ode to a Grecian Urn*.

The roundelay is a lovely lyric, breaking into and lightening the long progress of the rhymed ten-syllable couplets and has a delicacy all its own. As the fifth stanza runs,

JOHN KEATS: THE PRINCIPLE OF BEAUTY

> *To Sorrow,*
> *I bade good-morrow,*
> *And thought to leave her far away behind;*
> *But cheerly, cheerly,*
> *She loves me dearly;*
> *She is so constant, and so kind:*
> *I would deceive her*
> *And so leave her*
> *But ah! she is so constant and so kind.*

Again, later, as the Poem nears its conclusion – though as a story it has none – we find a passage where Keats's thought turns to the deeper side of life, again a foretaste of his grander, mature work. And so to Endymion's cry,

> *I have clung*
> *To nothing, lov'd a nothing, nothing seen*
> *Or felt but a great dream!*

and the happier beauty of

> *Still let me speak;*
> *Still let me dive into the joy I seek –*
> *For yet the past doth prison me. The rill,*
> *Thou haply mayst delight in, will I fill*
> *With pairs of fishes from the mountain tarn,*
> *And thou shalt feed them from the squirrel's barn.*
> *Its bottom will I strew with amber shells,*
> *And pebbles blue from deep enchanted wells.*
> *Its sides I'll plant with dew-sweet eglantine,*
> *And honey suckles full of clear bee-wine.*

It is for such lines, such fancies that *Endymion* lives, not for its labyrinthine story. Has any boy of twenty-two, before or since, ever written so? It was begun in the spring of 1817 at Carisbrooke, continued in the summer and early autumn in London and at Oxford, and finished in November at Burford Bridge. By February, 1818, the ardent, upward march of Keats's mind caused him to wish to 'forget it and proceed'.

And so into 1818, the year of *Isabella*, of the careful and thorough revision of *Endymion* (in itself a sufficient explanation of Keats's meaning about Poetry coming 'naturally'), its publication and the hostile attacks, the year of the Scottish tour with Charles Brown, ended by the catching of a severe cold in the Isle of Mull which, indubitably, germinated the latent seeds of consumption, the year of the beginning of *Hyperion*, of the meeting in the autumn with Fanny Brawne, who, incidentally, was only just eighteen, of the heart-tearing death in December of Tom, Keats's loved younger brother, who had 'an exquisite love of life', followed almost immediately by the engagement, on Christmas Day, to Fanny, the year on the threshold of enduring glory.

❦ III ❧

MORNING GLORY

KEATS was not as other men, even as other poets who, for the most part, zealously inscribe their productions in notebooks and keep them carefully, even anxiously: Keats wrote as and when he felt like it and was always mentally on the march, so that this upward surge coupled with his modesty rendered him almost indifferent to the fate of many of his lesser pieces – and of some of his greater also. He wrote, on October 27, 1818, to Woodhouse, 'I feel assured I should write from the mere yearning and fondness I have for the Beautiful even if my night's labours should be burnt every morning, and no eye ever shine upon them'. He could, and did, take infinite pains with his work as his labours on *Endymion* prove, and such a letter as that of his to John Taylor, Hessey's partner and his publisher, written in June, 1820 – if it stood alone, which it does not – amply attests his particularity of revision. But we owe the preservation of many poems that it would be a sad loss to forget, not to him but to the solicitude of his friends. No one else, it may be safely said, certainly no young, ambitious poet would have left uncollected, and sometimes unpublished even in a periodical, some of the poems which he either did not remember or did not bother to include in the 1820 volume: illness had gripped him, and he did not care – but the world has since shown it cared.

There is, for example, the sonnet *On the Sea* which Keats copied for Reynolds on April 17, 1817, from Carisbrooke, after mentioning that the relevant passage in Lear had 'haunted him intensely':

> It keeps eternal whisperings around
> Desolate shores, and with its mighty swell
> Gluts twice ten thousand caverns, till the spell
> Of Hecate leaves them their old shadowy sound.
> Often 'tis in such gentle temper found,
> That scarcely will the very smallest shell
> Be moved for days from where it sometime fell,
> When last the winds of heaven were unbound.
> Oh ye! who have your eyeballs vexed and tired,
> Feast them upon the wideness of the sea;
> Oh ye! whose ears are dinn'd with uproar rude,
> Or fed too much with cloying melody –
> Sit ye near some old cavern's mouth, and brood
> Until ye start, as if the sea-nymphs quired!

Though it has not the later mastery and he seemed either not to have noticed or not to have minded that the fourth line is of twelve syllables, it has peculiar beauty – and it also has special interest in that lines 6, 7 and 8 are direct forerunners of the lovely lines 7, 8, 9 and 10 of the opening of *Hyperion*:

> No stir of air was there,
> Not so much life as on a summer's day
> Robs not one light seed from the feather'd grass
> But where the dead leaf fell, there did it rest.

There are many such instances in Keats where he, as it were, foretells his future poetry: rapid, even exotic as was the growth of his power, it was nonetheless a natural, an inevitable growth, a ripening from bud to blossom and then to richest fruit. Attempts have been made to suggest that Fanny Brawne changed him – his poetry exists to disprove it: he developed – and magically – but he did not change.

The sonnet *To the Sea* was printed in *The Champion* of August 17, 1817, but no place was found for it in the 1820 volume: it first appeared in the *Literary Remains*, 1848.

The same exclusion befell the charming sonnet sent also to John Hamilton Reynolds ten months later – on February 18, 1818, when as Keats wrote, 'the beauty of the morning operated on a sense of idleness, adding that the thrush said he was right – 'seeming to say',

> *O thou whose face hath felt the Winter's wind*
> *Whose eye has seen the snow-clouds hung in mist,*
> *And the black elm tops 'mong the freezing stars,*
> *To thee the spring will be a harvest-time.*
> *O thou, whose only book has been the light*
> *Of supreme darkness which thou feddest on*
> *Night after night when Phoebus was away,*
> *To thee the spring shall be a triple morn.*
> *O fret not after knowledge – I have none,*
> *And yet my song comes native with the warmth.*
> *O fret not after knowledge – I have none,*
> *And yet the Evening listens. He who saddens*
> *At thoughts of idleness cannot be idle,*
> *And he's awake who thinks himself asleep.*

It would be possible to quote many other poems which had to wait until long after Keats's death to be known, poems which were written before the appearance of the third, and final, volume to be published in his lifetime: I will content myself here with only two more, one little known, the other world-famous. The first is one of six pieces described by the sedulous and devoted friends as *Fragments from an Opera* – of which the sixth and last will be given anon. This is the delicate, delicious little *Daisy's Song*, written, it is not known when but some time presumably in the spring in 1818 – there is, as Mr Maurice Buxton Forman points out, two lines similar to the ninth and tenth in the verse Keats inscribed for George and Georgiana Keats in his journal-letter of October, 1818, prophecying as to the birth of a nephew to be the first American poet, a prophecy not fulfilled:

> *The sun, with his great eye,*
> *Sees not so much as I;*
> *And the moon, all silver-proud,*
> *Might as well be in a cloud.*
>
> *And O the spring – the spring!*
> *I lead the life of a king!*
> *Couch'd in the teeming grass,*
> *I spy each pretty lass.*
>
> *I look where no one dares,*
> *And I stare where no one stares,*
> *And when the night is nigh,*
> *Lambs bleat my lullaby.*

Poetry is commonly felt to be without humour: here is proof to the contrary.

There is doubt about the date of writing of the second poem I will quote here: Miss Dorothy Hewlett says it was written at Burford Bridge as he was finishing *Endymion*, which he did on November 28, 1817. Professor Garrod in his edition of Keats's Poems, records that Reynolds has a pencil-note, 'Abt Oct. or Nov. 1818' and also that the date of the letter Woodhouse sent to Taylor, containing the transcript, was November 23, 1818. At all events, it was not printed until it was published in the Literary Gazette of September 18, 1829. It has never had a title.

In drear-nighted December,
　Too happy, happy tree,
Thy branches ne'er remember
　Their green felicity:
The north wind cannot undo them;
Nor frozen thawings glue them
　From budding at the prime.

In drear-nighted December,
　Too happy, happy brook,
Thy bubblings ne'er remember
　Apollo's summer look;
But with a sweet forgetting,
They stay their crystal fretting,
Never, never petting
　About the frozen time.

Ah! would 'twere so with many
　A gentle girl and boy!
But were there ever any
　Writh'd not at passed joy?
The feel of not to feel it,
When there is none to heal it,
Nor numbed sense to steel it,
　Was never said in rhyme.

MORNING GLORY

World-famous as the lines are, I give them in full because they represent the one case where I do not print lines quoted from Keats in the form in which they are given by Professor Garrod: his edition is definite and exact, but here he has decided to part company with Keats's preference. This he admits in his introduction, adding that Woodhouse confessed to 'an utter abhorrence' of the fifth line of the third stanza as usually given, namely,

> To know the change and feel it.

Professor Garrod says this is 'both better poetry and better logic': it may be so, but we know that Keats wrote the other, which may not be so 'elegant' – to use Sir Sidney Colvin's word – but seems to have quite a different, and – if I may diffidently say so – a much more original meaning. That *The Gazette* printed the emendation hardly matters, unless it can be proved that that was with Keats's approval. In its revised version the poem has passed for one of Keats's finest successes. But to say that it was snatched out of failure, as Professor Garrod says, snatched, that is, by this alteration is to express an opinion in which I, for one, cannot follow him.

And, since the text, as here given, is as written by Keats, let us omit the unnecessary, and weakening, 'a' in the first line of Stanzas I and II: it is preferable, surely, both as metre and sense.

There are many others, not included in the 1820 volume, and a number which have come to light since the 1848 *Remains* – such as,

> I had a dove and the sweet dove died,

and the rhymed letter to Reynolds, with its foretaste of the Odes, first, *To a Grecian Urn*, where Keats writes,

> *The sacrifice goes on; the pontiff knife*
> *Gleams in the sun, the milk-white heifer lows,*

and also,

> *Things cannot to the will*
> *Be settled, but they tease us out of thought;*

and, secondly, to the *Ode on Melancholy* in the lines,

> *It is a flaw*
> *In happiness to see beyond our bourn –*
> *It forces us in Summer skies to mourn:*
> *It spoils the singing of the Nightingale.*

It cannot be over-emphasized that Keats's work is all of a piece throughout the whole of his poetic life: it is a profound mistake to think otherwise; his threads of thought run unbrokenly.

But it is time to pass from these fugitive pieces, however interesting or beautiful they may be. Keats was a boy no longer: the labour of *Endymion* had ripened him like a sun, and he was ready for the Poems on which his throne is reared. Almost ready, for, though it is a part, and no small part, of the great 1820 volume, *Isabella* or *The Pot of Basil* is still not Keats the fully ripened, the assured master of poetic art.

Isabella stands midway both in date and in poetic achievement between his early luxuriance and the disciplined majesty of his maturity; and, like many mid-way things, it has been variously regarded. To Charles Lamb it was the most important poem in the 1820 volume – which contains the *Odes* and *Hyperion*: to Mr Middleton Murry, whose judgment here is not affected by any thought of Fanny Brawne, it is 'the least important of all Keats's long poems whatsoever': it has won, at all events, its way to wider popularity than the others by reason, presumably, of the straight and limpid current of its narrative.

In this tale, based directly upon one from Boccaccio, Keats sets a limit to his luxuriance – though a word may here be fitly said about this quality: he is at all times rich in imaginative detail, copious to a marvellous degree, but, most poetic of poets as he is, he never indulges in poetic verbiage. He never, as Tennyson did, would have written 'ocean-spoil in ocean-smelling osier' if he had wished to describe fish in a fish-basket, or 'the knightly growth that fringed his lips' as the description of a moustache. His descriptions, however poetic, are direct, and drawn from direct and minute observation. But in his early fecundity the wealth and variety of his imagery clogs the progress of his verse. *Isabella* marks the transition when he was learning control and gaining in dramatic power.

Isabella, accordingly, does not wander here, there, and everywhere like a bee in a bower, as *Endymion* does: it follows, in the main, the story of Boccaccio; but this story, for all the veil of Poetry that Keats seeks to throw over it – and does throw, for the most part, with wonderful delicacy of touch – is macabre, and even unpleasant: it is not a theme deserving of such honour and not all Keats's skill can make it so. The good novelist's power of structural building is not where Keats excels: the same, no doubt, has been said of Shakespeare who borrowed plots with opulent carelessness. In four at any rate of Keats's long poems, *Endymion, Isabella, Lamia* and the *Eve of St Agnes* a weakness, or at least an inconsistency, is to be found: in the first three it matters materially; in the fourth, magically, it seems to possess no significance.

In *Isabella* Keats has set himself the task of fusing into Poetry the treacherous murder of a man, the digging up and severing of his head by the young girl who loved him, who puts it in her pot of basil and then waters and tends it as her most prized treasure until the murderers, her brothers, steal the pot, examine it, discover its horrid contents and flee, leaving her to pine away and die – no Poetry can transmute the unpleasantness and the reader must be forgiven if he cries, with Keats,

> *Ah! wherefore all this wormy circumstance?*

If anyone could have succeeded, it would have been Keats, for the poem has, inevitably in his hands, lovely lines and a disarming simplicity of beauty, as, for instance, Stanza X, the sweetness of the love of Lorenzo and Isabella before doom fell upon them:

> *Parting they seem'd to tread upon the air,*
> *Twin roses by the zephyr blown apart*
> *Only to meet again more close, and share*
> *The inward fragrance of each other's heart.*
> *She, to her chamber gone, a ditty fair*
> *Sang, of delicious love and honey'd dart;*
> *He with light steps went up a western hill,*
> *And bade the sun farewell, and joy'd his fill.*

MORNING GLORY

or Stanza LIII, when Isabella returns with her treasure:

> And she forgot the stars, the moon, and sun,
>   And she forgot the blue above the trees,
> And she forgot the dells where waters run,
>   And she forgot the chilly autumn breeze;
> She had no knowledge when the day was done,
>   And the new moon she saw not: but in peace
> Hung over her sweet basil evermore,
> And moisten'd it with tears unto the core.

The dramatic anticipation,

> So the two brothers and their murder'd man
> Rode past fair Florence,

was specially commended by Lamb and is a step forward in Keats's mastery to date. *Isabella* belongs to Teignmouth and the spring of 1818. Earlier, in happy mood, he had written the merry *Robin Hood* and *Mermaid* lines to John Hamilton Reynolds, the first, as he said 'written in the spirit of Outlawry'. Instances, both, of genius stretching her wings preparatory to flights into the empyrean, included in the 1820 volume in the midst of the *Odes* – all except the fragmentary *Ode to Maia* written on May 1, 1818, the publication of which had to wait for 1848; it is one of the earliest examples of the work of Keats at its loveliest:

> Mother of Hermes! and still youthful Maia!
>   May I sing to thee
> As thou wast hymned on the shores of Baiae?
>   Or may I woo thee
> In earlier Sicilian? or thy smiles
> Seek as they once were sought, in Grecian isles,
> By bards who died content on pleasant sward,

JOHN KEATS: THE PRINCIPLE OF BEAUTY

> Leaving great verse unto a little clan?
> O, give me their old vigour, and unheard
>   Save of the quiet Primrose, and the span
>   Of heaven and few ears,
> Rounded by thee, my song should die away,
>   Content as theirs,
> Rich in the simple worship of a day.

a fragment to which Swinburne gave the word 'divine'.

Keats could not live without Poetry, but periods of giving out alternated, naturally and almost inevitably, with periods of taking in, and the summer of 1818 was not a productive period. He was very much alone in his heart these days, Tom was ill, Fanny a child under the constraint of the Abbeys, George, of whom Keats said he 'always stood between me and any dealing with the world', left in June for America with Georgiana Wylie, now his bride, Fanny Brawne was in the future: the tour to the Lakes and Scotland with Brown filled the summer months. It is, perhaps, a little surprising that this did not fill Keats's later poems with illustrative descriptions: the view over 'Winandermere' had a special appeal to his sense of Beauty. He wrote a few sonnets such as *On Visiting the Tomb of Burns*, and *Ailsa Rock*, and some fugitive pieces for Tom, Fanny, and Bailey, *Meg Merrilies* and 'a song about himself'; *There was a naughty Boy*, *There is a joy in footing slow across a silent plain*, and other lines; but these are almost all, apart from the beginning of *Hyperion* – a tremendous addition, which will be dealt with later. Keats returned to Hampstead, seriously unwell, to face the winter of the critical attacks, the meeting with Fanny Brawne, and Tom's death, followed by his engagement.

MORNING GLORY

And so we pass to the *annus mirabilis*, 1819 – and yet for all the wonder of Keats's poetic achievement in this year, his twenty-fourth, especially in the first half of it, the happiest time of his life, it is not an unexpected wonder: it is a growth. We know that fruit comes from blossom, and we can by analysis and science expound, even if we cannot explain, the process – so is it with Keats. The majesty of his greatest poems written, for the most part, in the spring of 1819, is inherent, undeveloped or budding, in his earlier.

Included in the 1820 volume, embedded in the midst of the great *Odes*, written presumably late in 1818, 'are one or two little poems you might like', writes Keats simply to George and Georgiana on January 2, 1819, and copies the two that, similar to the *Robin Hood* and *Mermaid* lines, are in the most difficult of English metres, that of *L'Allegro* and *Il Penseroso*, the first beginning

> *Ever let the fancy roam*
> *Pleasure never is at home:*
> *At a touch sweet pleasure melteth,*
> *Like to bubbles where rain pelteth;*
> *Then let winged Fancy wander,*

and the second

> *Bards of Passion and of Mirth*
> *Ye have left your souls on earth!*
> *Have ye souls in heaven too,*
> *Double-lived in regions new?*

Keats added in his letter, 'these are specimens of a sort of rondeau which I think I shall become partial to': but he was destined for greater measures.

JOHN KEATS: THE PRINCIPLE OF BEAUTY

But, first, before he comes to the stanza form of his perfecting, there is a reversion to the Spenserian. There is something so naïve, so modest as in the light of the world's opinion to be almost ludicrous in his first announcement of this to George and Georgiana, in his letter begun on Sunday morning, February 14, 1819, at Wentworth Place. He had been down to stay first with Dilke's father at Chichester and then with Dilke's sister at Bedhampton. 'Nothing worth speaking of,' he writes, 'happened at either place. I took down some thin paper and wrote on it a little poem call'd St Agnes' Eve.' Was ever the announcement of a fact about which the world has spoken continuously made in such a fashion? One could love Keats for those two sentences alone.

The Eve of St Agnes – to give it the title and the form in which it was printed in 1820 – is, it can be said without much fear of challenge, the first of Keats's really great completed poems. Its appeal is quite irresistible. 'It is,' says Mr M. R. Ridley at the outset of his detailed technical examination in his *Keats's Craftsmanship*, 'the deliberate work of a trained craftsman': it is much more, of course, than that; no training, craftsmanship, or deliberation can produce magic, even though the magician needs must be trained before he can achieve his best effects. It is, however it is looked at, a very singular poem. Its story, like those of *Endymion*, *Isabella*, and *Lamia*, is tenuous – or worse, and is marred by a grievous inconsistency, two inconsistencies rather. The first of these two lies in the character and action of the principal performer, Porphyro. Paul Pry and Peeping Tom are, by general consent, two of the most ignoble characters in immemorial story-telling: yet Porphyro, Keats's hero, takes a leaf out of their book in this tale. He over-persuades old Angela, 'weak', as she is described, 'in body and in soul', to let him spy upon Madeleine, his beloved, as she undresses, which, as one well versed in poetry once said succinctly, is 'disgusting'. But, more than that, Porphyro in Stanza XVII makes Angela a solemn promise:

> '*I will not harm her, by all saints I swear,*'
> *Quoth Porphyro:* '*O may I ne'er find grace*
> '*When my weak voice shall whisper its last prayer*
> '*If one of her soft ringlets I displace,*
> '*Or look with ruffian passion in her face:*
> '*Good Angela, believe me by these tears.*'

Good Angela does believe him – and he does not keep his promise. He not only looks 'with ruffian passion', but he certainly displaces Madeleine's 'soft ringlets'.

That is the second inconsistency about which there was prompt controversy, argument, and disagreement. Keats had made it plain that the union between the two lovers was to be a real one and, though in deference to the protests of Woodhouse and his publishers, he left it vague still he maintained that the 'solution sweet' of Stanza XXXVI was in reality explicit.

It is hardly possible to believe that, whatever Porphyro's action, Madeleine's mind remained in dream: and the 'solution sweet' of Keats's intention therefore seems to render inconsistent his description of her,

> *She knelt, so pure a thing, so free from mortal taint,*

one of the most hauntingly lovely lines in the poem.

All this would prove – as, indeed, inconsistency in Lamia's story proves – a fatal flaw to the enjoyment of the poem if reality could be anywhere attached to it. Happily, it cannot. And the proof lies in a single alteration. Towards the end when 'morning is at hand' (almost a reminiscence, perhaps, of the exquisite parting of Romeo and Juliet) Porphyro cries

> *Awake! arise! my love, and fearless be,*
> *For o'er the southern moors I have a home for thee.*

The alternative was 'over the Dartmoor black' – an obvious topographical description derived from Keats's stay at Teignmouth. Its effect, if that had been in the final version, would be to bring the whole story down to earth. As it is, it is pure faery – and earth-bound moralities and inconsistencies have no part or place in it at all.

Keats himself never thought very highly of the poem: Mr Ridley writes, 'in its kind, even though that kind be slight, it is not far short of perfection' – a very odd sentence: it is not easy to understand how any one, whether praising or detracting, could think of the kind as 'slight'. It has a warmth and a wonder about it which is the very essence of poetic enchantment, from the eery, unexpected start,

> *St Agnes' Eve – Ah, bitter chill it was!*
> *The owl, for all his feathers, was a-cold,*

to its equally eery, unexpected conclusion,

> *The Beadsman, after thousand aves told,*
> *For aye unsought for slept among his ashes cold,*

the original conclusion infinitely preferable to a later, satirical emendation.

MORNING GLORY

The whole of it is endlessly rich in magic and every reader will find his or her own delight. Apart from whole passages of loveliness and wealth of warm, rich lines there are so many entrancing sudden expressions as, for example, 'the silver, snarling trumpets', 'dwarfish Hildebrand', 'her warmed jewels', 'an azure-lidded sleep', 'the tiger moth's deep-damask'd wings' – there are beauties innumerable that 'beggar all description'.

Immediately after first writing this glorious fantasy, Keats turned to the quiet and lovely fragment, another *Eve* that of *St Mark*. It is medieval and marvellously serene; 'a little thing', Keats called it and, after copying it out for George and Georgiana in September, wrote he hoped they would 'like it for all its Carelessness' – of which quality is no trace unless he means its ease. Keats's openings are almost always supremely good: this is no exception:

Upon a Sabbath-day it fell;
Twice holy was the Sabbath-bell
That call'd the folk to evening prayer.

Like other great work of his, it was not included in the 1820 volume, presumably because it was yet another fragment, and it had to await publication till 1848.

From it we rise on to the topmost pinnacles, but in that ascent should pause briefly to touch upon five pieces, preludes to the mountain ranges, all as different as could be imagined – and in their difference lies much. None belong to the 1820 volume: all belong to literary history and one to the whole world. The first is the sonnet of which Keats says in March, 1819, to George and Georgiana it was written 'with no agony but that of ignorance; with no thirst of anything but knowledge', though he adds, 'I wrote with my mind – and perhaps I must confess a little bit of my heart':

> *Why did I laugh to-night? No voice will tell:*
> *No God, no Demon of severe response,*
> *Deigns to reply from heaven or from Hell.*
> *Then to my human heart I turn at once.*
> *Heart! Thou and I are here sad and alone;*
> *I say, why did I laugh? O mortal pain!*
> *O Darkness! Darkness! ever must I moan,*
> *To question Heaven and Hell and Heart in vain.*
> *Why did I laugh? I know this Being's lease,*
> *My fancy to its utmost blisses spreads;*
> *Yet would I on this very midnight cease,*
> *And the world's gaudy ensigns see in shreds;*
> *Verse, Fame, and Beauty are intense indeed,*
> *But Death intenser – Death is Life's high need.*

Keats records that, having written this, he 'went to bed and enjoyed an uninterrupted sleep'. That is interesting, and there are two other features of interest – apart, that is, from the power of the poetry which is incontestable. One is that the eleventh line is a direct forerunner of Stanza VI of the world-famous *Ode to a Nightingale*, soon to be born, the other that the sonnet has been interpreted to suggest Keats's agony of mind and heart at this date. The objection to that is threefold: first, his own words, which Miss Dorothy Hewlett cannot bring herself to believe, secondly, that at this date Keats, though still grieving for Tom, was at his happiest, and thirdly, that it comes in the journal-letter of March-April, 1819, shortly before the 'little extempore', beginning,

MORNING GLORY

> *When they were come into the Faery's Court*
> *They rang – no one at home – all gone to sport*
> *And dance and kiss and love as faeries do*
> *For Faeries be as humans, lovers true*

(printed by Professor Garrod among *Trivia* at his edition's end) and that that is followed, next day, April 16, that is, by excellently jocular lines on Charles Brown, beginning,

> *He is to weet a melancholy carle:*
> *Thin in the waist, with bushy head of hair,*
> *As hath the seeded thistle when in parle*
> *It holds the Zephyr, ere it sendeth fair*
> *Its light balloons into the summer air.*

'It is clear,' writes Mr Middleton Murry of the sonnet, 'that the laugh had been one of cynical despair:' there is not much evidence of cynicism in Keats – as yet – if his letter can be taken at all to mean what it contains: and why, why should it not be?

The fourth of these pieces is the sonnet, *As Hermes once*, which was printed in *The Indicator* of June 28, 1820: it was written in April, 1818, after a dream, 'one of the most delightful enjoyments I ever had in my life,' says Keats, and is of peculiar interest for its conclusion which runs,

> *Pale were the sweet lips I saw,*
> *Pale were the lips I kiss'd, and fair the form*
> *I floated with, about that melancholy storm.*

That leads directly to the fifth, probably the most famous – and certainly the most controversial – of Keats's poems. A few pages after the sonnet, Keats writes in for his brother and sister-in-law, without an introductory or explanatory word, *La Belle Dame sans merci*. This, like the last, was printed in *The Indicator* of May 10, 1820, but also not included in the 1820 volume, a singular omission, as it now seems.

It has become one of the best-known poems in the world. 'This,' exclaimed William Morris, as he corrected the proofs for his Kelmscott Press edition of Keats, 'was the germ from which all the poetry of my group has sprung!' On the other side may be set the quiet, skilled judgment of Francis Palgrave, 'Keats is not quite at his best, not quite himself, in this imitative Ballad – which, alone among his poems, is admirable rather for the picturesqueness of the whole than (as with *Lamia* or the *Nightingale*) for the equal wealth of the details also.' I set that down because, in spite of the strange, unearthly beauty of the poem's music, it seems to me just.

But it is necessary now to quote, and, I fear, disagree with, another most eminent critic, Mr Middleton Murry. He says, without equivocation, that behind both these last two poems 'is the anguish of an impossible love. La Belle Dame is Fanny Brawne' – which, I have to say, seems to me a wholly unjustified piece of unsupported imagination. But that is not quite all. The poem which begins, as most readers will remember, with the question,

>   O what can ail thee, knight-at-arms,
>   Alone and palely loitering?
>   The sedge has wither'd from the lake,
>   And no birds sing,

has the following eighth stanza

MORNING GLORY

> *She took me to her elfin grot,*
>   *And there she wept, and sigh'd full sore,*
> *And there I shut her wild wild eyes*
>   *With kisses four.*

Keats adds to George and Georgiana the following explanatory comment, 'Why four kisses – you will say – why four? because I wish to restrain the headlong impetuosity of my Muse – she would have fain said 'score' without hurting the rhyme – but we must temper the Imagination as the critics say with Judgment. I was obliged to choose an even number that both eyes might have fair play: and to speak truly I think two a piece quite sufficient. Suppose I had said seven; there would have been three and a half a piece – a very awkward affair and well got out of on my side.'

Those are Keats's own words: they seem to me to be wholly in keeping with the humorous, human, modest man we know him to have been, his reaction, characteristic of English folk, against anything high-brow. But they are torn to shreds by Mr Murry who, after quoting these words, says, 'That is not the bitter detachment of the laugh of *Why did I laugh to-night?* It is the detachment of a man who has uttered his heart and must turn away from what he has said. It is the irony of the pain of self-revelation: it is the irony of Hamlet, the unembittered irony of the soul which begins to see beyond its pain, and to comprehend that the pain must be.'

Readers can decide for themselves whether Keats meant this or whether he meant what he wrote, bearing in mind that in April, 1819, Keats was not an unhappy, hopeless man; he was not well and he was very poor, but he was a young man passionately in love and at his greatest heights of poetry. And I might, perhaps, just add this: 'if the dame hadn't had mercy,' said a very witty lady laughingly to me, 'she would never have allowed as many kisses as four.' It seems a comment at least as well attuned to Keats's own words as the straining after the cynical and the macabre, a straining which would assuredly have brought laughter, if not scorn, to those sensitive lips of Keats. Why, why drag in 'detachment, irony, and pain'?

The two well-known sonnets on *Fame* and the quiet, lovely sonnet *To Sleep*, followed on April 30. I quote the latter, one more not published in 1820, as a proof of the serenity of Keats's mind at this date.

> *O soft embalmer of the still midnight,*
> *Shutting, with careful fingers and benign,*
> *Our gloom-pleas'd eyes, embowered from the light,*
> *Enshaded in forgetfulness divine;*
> *O soothest Sleep! if so it please thee, close,*
> *In midst of this thine hymn, my willing eyes,*
> *Or wait the amen, ere thy poppy throws*
> *Around my bed its lulling charities;*
> *Then save me, or the passed day will shine*
> *Upon my pillow, breeding many woes;*
> *Save me from curious conscience, that still lords*
> *Its strength for darkness, burrowing like a mole;*
> *Turn the key deftly in the oiled wards,*
> *And seal the hushed casket of my soul.*

That has – to my ear at least – as no other poem quite has, the same enchanting quietude of music as the poem *To Autumn*. And fittingly it heralds in the majesty of the five *Odes* which belong to this spring of 1819, the work of which might well be termed miraculous if that word did not suggest a change in character from work which preceded it. Change there was in power, in music, in grandeur – but not change in character: that cannot be emphasized sufficiently.

Keats wrote ten Poems to which the word 'Ode' is ascribed – though the ascription is rather eclectic, being given to the *Ode on Melancholy* but not *To Autumn*: of these three are of minor importance, two to Apollo and one to Fanny; a fourth and fifth are the fragment to *Maia* and *Bards of Passion and of Mirth*, both already quoted. Five remain, all written in April and May, 1819. These constitute (with one addition) the highest peaks not only of Keats's Poetry but of all Poetry in the English language, with the single exception of Shakespeare's at his best; and they are the product of the mind of one who was only twenty-three and a half years old. It is pleasant to be here in fullest agreement with Mr Middleton Murry, Fanny Brawne not being brought by him seriously into question – though he does not explain his omission, which would seem entirely to invalidate his theory as to the evil of her influence on Keats's mind.

Of them Swinburne wrote (including *To Autumn*), 'greater lyrical poetry the world may have seen than any that is in these; lovelier it surely has never seen, nor can it possibly see.'

These *Odes* present any writer on Keats, accordingly, with a very real dilemma. To say anything fresh or interesting of poems which have been interminably quoted, read, recited, and dissected in every part of the globe is to tax ingenuity to the uttermost: to say nothing of them is impossible. They are the everlasting hills of Keats's delectable land of Poetry: remove them and for all the loveliness of so much of the rest of his work, he would remain unknown to all

JOHN KEATS: THE PRINCIPLE OF BEAUTY

but a very few. It is in four of these *Odes* and *To Autumn* – and only in these for the vast mass of Mankind – that he lives and will live perdurably.

The four are *Ode to Psyche, Ode on Melancholy, Ode on a Grecian Urn* and *Ode to a Nightingale*. The fifth, *Ode on Indolence*, was not included in the 1820 volume and has never won universal acclamation, though Keats wrote to Miss Jeffrey on June 9, 1819, that writing it had been the thing he had most enjoyed that year. This might well be pleasant frivolity to a friend but the *Ode* is not in the same class of beauty as its four sisters – though Robert Bridges ranked it as high: its form is generally that of three of the great *Odes*, Keats's perfected invention, a Shakespearean quatrain followed by a Petrarchan sextet, to make a stanza. But each has variations, and *To Autumn* is different again. The first of the four to be written, the *Ode to Psyche* is – as far as metre goes – experimental.

It is, however, not the purpose of this book to enter into a technical discussion on prosody or to analyze and dissect metrical design: Professor Garrod has an illuminating passage in his Introduction to Keats's Poetry on this studying of the craftsmanship, defending it in the case of the immortals and adding, 'The only likely damage is what we may do to ourselves: in all study of technique we risk *our own* poetry.'

This is the fifth of the six stanzas of the *Ode on Indolence*:

> And once more came they by; – alas! wherefore?
> My sleep had been embroider'd with dim dreams;
> My soul had been a lawn besprinkled o'er
> With flowers, and stirring shades, and baffled beams:
> The morn was clouded, but no shower fell,
> Tho' in her lids hung the sweet tears of May;

MORNING GLORY

> *The open casement press'd a new-leav'd vine,*
> *Let in the budding warmth and throstle's lay;*
> *O Shadows! 'twas a time to bid farewell!*
> *Upon your skirts had fallen no tears of mine.*

Delicate, charming even – but of a surety lacking the magic of what the world agrees are the great *Odes*.

But it has a recognizable affinity in thought and expression with the *Ode to Psyche* and its radiant conclusion,

> *And in the midst of this wide quietness*
> *A rosy sanctuary will I dress*
> *With the wreath'd trellis of a working brain,*
> *With buds, and bells, and stars without a name,*
> *With all the gardener Fancy e'er could feign,*
> *Who breeding flowers, will never breed the same:*
> *And there shall be for thee all soft delight*
> *That shadowy thought can win,*
> *A bright torch, and a casement ope at night,*
> *To let the warm Love in!*

How fond Keats was not only of flowers, as has been already noted, but of casements! 'The stars through the window pane are my Children,' as he said; and his favourite seat was by the window, as his friends knew.

The reverse, after shadowy thought has won, may, perhaps, be found in lines 10-12 of the quietly beautiful sonnet *The Day is gone*, also of 1819 – but later (again not published till 1848):

> *When the dusk holiday – or holinight*
> *Of fragrant-curtain'd love begins to weave*
> *The woof of darkness thick, for hid delight.*

JOHN KEATS: THE PRINCIPLE OF BEAUTY

This *Ode to Psyche* has interest over and above its deep, warm beauty. Miss Dorothy Hewlett says it was written in May, 1819; but it is generally held to be earlier, the first of the four. It is set down by Keats for George and Georgiana in his journal-letter, in the section dated April 30, and was therefore written before that. It leads on metrically to the others and Keats's own comments support that. First he says that it 'is first and the only one with which I have taken even moderate pains. I have for the most part dash'd off my lines in a hurry', and then, after copying it out, he adds, 'I have been endeavouring to discover a better Sonnet Stanza than we have'; and so to the two *Odes* familiar to all readers of English Poetry, young, middle-aged, and old, the world over, the *Ode on a Grecian Urn* and the *Ode to a Nightingale;* also to the third, the *Ode on Melancholy*, which the world knows less – though its fame is world-wide also.

It is some measure of the greatness of the work of Keats in these two magical spring months of April and May, 1819, that even the most eminent of critics have disputed and differed as to the order of merit in which the *Odes* should be placed – some placing one first, some another – but all place all as high as Poetry can be placed. They are too familiar to be set down yet again here. It is enough to draw attention once again to the continuity of thought and even expression in Keats's life. On March 25, 1818, he had written from Teignmouth to John Hamilton Reynolds a letter in verse, beginning very simply,

Dear Reynolds, as last night I lay in bed,

which – also – was never published till 1848: did ever any poet leave more 'literary remains'?

MORNING GLORY

Lines 20-22 of this poetical epistle run:

> *The sacrifice goes on; the pontiff knife*
> *Gleams in the sun, the milk-white heifer lows,*
> *The pipes go shrilly, the libation flows.*

As all will remember, the fourth stanza of the *Ode on a Grecian Urn* begins,

> *Who are these coming to the sacrifice?*
> *To what green altar, O mysterious priest,*
> *Lead'st thou that heifer lowing at the skies,*
> *And all his silken flanks with garlands drest?*

Lines 76-77 of the epistle to Reynolds run,

> *Things cannot to the will*
> *Be settled, but they tease us out of thought,*

and lines 4-5 of Stanza V of the *Urn* are,

> *Thou, silent form, dost tease us out of thought*
> *As doth eternity.*

Similarly lines 82-84 of the epistle are:

> *It is a flaw*
> *In happiness to see beyond our bourn —*
> *It forces us in Summer skies to mourn:*
> *It spoils the singing of the Nightingale.*

That has in it not only the thought latent in much of the *Ode to the Nightingale* but more definitely that of the lovely,

JOHN KEATS: THE PRINCIPLE OF BEAUTY

lovely third stanza of the *Ode on Melancholy*, which I quote for loveliness's sake alone, familiar as it must be to all my readers:

> She dwells with Beauty — Beauty that must die;
> And Joy, whose hand is ever at his lips
> Bidding adieu; and aching Pleasure nigh,
> Turning to poison while the bee-mouth sips:
> Ay, in the very temple of Delight
> Veil'd Melancholy has her sovran shrine,
> Though seen of none save him whose strenuous tongue
> Can burst Joy's grape against his palate fine;
> His soul shall taste the sadness of her might,
> And be among her cloudy trophies hung.

Some times I have noticed the double sound of 'among' and 'hung', and wished that that had been avoided as, for instance, by 'amid' for 'among'; but then I have remembered the saying of an eminent critic of music and literature, Sir Henry Hadow, 'Great artists do not blunder into beauty', and reflected that either Keats deliberately chose to have that assonance in his final line, in which case every living critic would admit that Keats's choice is more likely to be good than his, or, alternatively, that he did not mind it, in which case no one else need. It is, indeed, almost impossible to imagine Poetry with richer music, deeper enchantment, or more perfect harmony of thought and expression: and with those lines, accordingly, I close this brief survey of Keats's morning glory. There is glory yet to come; but it is not morning glory. Young as he was, he could say with truth unequalled and far deeper than his meaning in December, 1818, 'Time is nothing — two years are as long as twenty'.

IV

SUNSET

SOMETHING of that which was as a flame of fire in the heart, mind, and body of Keats can be seen from a few words of his, written in the letter to Miss Jeffry on June 9, 1819 from which the statement of his enjoyment in writing the *Ode on Indolence* has been already quoted. Two sentences before that he writes, 'I have been very idle lately, very averse to writing; both from the overpowering idea of our dead poets and from abatement of my love of fame.' When the magnitude both in power, variety, and extent, of his production during the weeks immediately preceding this is considered the statement gives some idea of his idea of Indolence. Never, never has any poet done so much in so short a space of time!

Flame of fire may be wonderful: it is also destructive; and Keats had the seeds of death in him. These, doubtless, were in part at least the cause of the fierceness of activity which was his. Poetry and Love, twin goddesses of his being, gave him no rest. He was poor and he was ailing, and marriage was a goal he recognized as impossible – he, let it be observed, not Fanny Brawne who never took that view, though she might well have done so: nor did her mother, in whom such a course of common sense clearly would have been abundantly justified. On the contrary, both mother and daughter showed a quite remarkable understanding and solicitude.

From September, 1818, to his death eighteen months later, there was no such thing as Indolence or ease or rest or quietude for Keats – though for the first twelve months of that time there was some happiness and the wonder of great Poetry. In the weeks preceding his letter to Miss Jeffry he had not only written a number of individual Poems, the longest of which was 80 lines, which tower like mountain ranges to the everlasting snows; he had not only written *The Eve of St Agnes*, 378 lines, and *The Eve of St Mark*, 119 lines, as well as a number of other little pieces, almost, as it were, casually, such as *La Belle Dame sans merci* and many sonnets: but – as if this was not more, much more than so young a mind had ever written before – he had also been writing a poem known to us as *Hyperion: A Fragment*. This he had begun in September, 1818, and it was continued until he laid it aside in April, 1819.

I have purposely left *Hyperion* on one side until now. It is difficult, even perhaps impossible, to keep precisely to chronology when a long poem – extending in its period of composition, over a number of months – is in question, though chronology is always important in a poet's life, and it is, obviously, particularly so in the case of one whose growth was at once so tremendous and so swift.

Hyperion was begun in September, 1818; by then he had – as he wrote on September 22 to Reynolds – 'relapsed into those abstractions which are my only life.' It was ominous that two sentences later he added, 'There is an awful warmth about my heart like a load of Immortality.' He was terribly anxious about Tom, and the cold he had brought back from Scotland oppressed him – though he could say, 'I shall soon be quite recovered.' He worked at *Hyperion* off and on for months; it was in process of composition all through the zenith of his power, during Tom's last illness, during the early weeks of his engagement, during the time of the writing of the *Odes*: it belongs, therefore, to the brief period of his greatest happiness overshadowed only by Tom's death and by his own consciousness of ill-health.

It was not until a year exactly after the letter to Reynolds just quoted that – on September 22, 1819 – he wrote to the same friend the well known words, 'I have given up Hyperion – there are too many Miltonic inversions in it – Miltonic verse cannot be written but in an artful or rather artist's humour. I wish to give myself up to other sensations. English ought to be kept up.' What is there in this, or the facts of Keats's life and production at this stage, to cause Mr Middleton Murry to write, 'There is no sadder poem in English than *Hyperion?*' Of personal sadness there is no trace: it deals undeniably with the twilight of the Titans, and about them there is accordingly a grave, dignified, majestic silence, but they are altogether too remote, in spite of all Keats's skill, from the realities of the modern world to make the reader sad with them – indeed, it is for that very reason that the poem was abandoned. To read personal history into it is to deny to Keats all power of inventiveness, especially as we know that the writing of the story of Hyperion was a project he had long contemplated.

And yet, fragmentary as it is, there is a singular glory about *Hyperion:* there is a gravity of melody, a depth of richness in it almost unapproachable, particularly in its opening which is of Keats's very greatest:

> *Deep in the shady sadness of a vale*
> *Far sunken from the healthy breath of morn,*
> *Far from the fiery noon, and eve's one star*
> *Sat gray-hair'd Saturn, quiet as a stone,*
> *Still as the silence round about his lair;*

> *Forest on forest hung above his head,*
> *Like cloud on cloud. No stir of air was there,*
> *Not so much life as on a summer's day*
> *Robs not one light seed from the feather'd grass*
> *But where the dead leaf fell, there did it rest.*
> *A stream went voiceless by, still deadened more*
> *By reason of his fallen divinity*
> *Spreading a shade: the Naiad 'mid her reeds*
> *Press'd her cold finger closer to his lips*
>   *Along the margin-sand large foot-marks went,*
> *No further than to where his feet had stray'd,*
> *And slept there since. Upon the sodden ground*
> *His old right hand lay nerveless, listless, dead,*
> *Unsceptred; and his realmless eyes were closed;*
> *While his bow'd head seem'd list'ning to the Earth,*
> *His ancient mother, for some comfort yet.*

Keats, writing blank verse for the first time in his life, achieves straight off an almost peerless melody and mastery: he was then twenty-three and a half.

The opening is too powerful, too great in simplicity and music to be sustained; and it is the highest point of the whole story. Not even Keats could give reality

> *To that large utterance of the early gods.*

But there is splendour, majestic twilight and harmony throughout, with such a tenderness as Milton has but which few, save Keats, have associated with that stern poet, as when at the end of Book I Coelus whispers 'low and solemn' to Hyperion:

SUNSET

'I am but a voice;
'My life is but the life of winds and tides,
'No more than winds and tides can I avail: —
'But thou canst. — Be thou therefore in the van
'Of Circumstance; yea, seize the arrow's barb
'Before the tense string murmur. — To the earth!
'For there thou wilt find Saturn, and his woes.
'Meantime I will keep watch on thy bright sun,
'And of thy seasons be a careful nurse.' —
Ere half this region-whisper had come down,
Hyperion arose, and on the stars
Lifted his curved lids, and kept them wide
Until it ceas'd; and still he kept them wide:
And still they were the same bright, patient stars.

Later, in Book II, comes the noble declaration of Oceanus,

> to bear all naked truths,
> And to envisage circumstance, all calm,
> That is the top of sovereignty.

This, in Keats's life, seems analogous to Hamlet's

> Give me the man that is not passion's slave.

After the Titans' debate, after

> The nightingale had ceas'd, and a few stars
> Were lingering in the heavens, while the thrush
> Began calm-throated,

Mnemosyne comes to the God of the Sun, and the poem breaks off abruptly with these lines:

JOHN KEATS: THE PRINCIPLE OF BEAUTY

> *At length*
> *Apollo shriek'd; and lo! from all his limbs*
> *Celestial....................*

In Woodhouse's transcript this last sentence is finished in pencil, '*glory dawn'd: he was a god!*' Mr Middleton Murry makes two categorical statements: first, that Apollo is none other than Keats himself, and, second, that the poem had to end where it did: 'it is the history of his own soul that is being unfolded.' 'Keats,' says Mr Murry, 'did not intend it to be continued.' The first statement rests solely in the illimitable realm of imagination; and, as for the second, personally I prefer Keats's explanation: it seems a little difficult to believe that he ought not to be considered the best, indeed the only judge of why he abandoned the poem.

There is no need to pursue this: the passion for interpretation can be carried to absurdity. The world in general is agreed on two things, that Keats was right to abandon *Hyperion* in that it was leading nowhere and that it is of singular magnificence. Shelley, as we know, cared little for Keats's other poems in the 1820 volume, but his judgment was that 'if the *Hyperion* be not grand poetry, none has been produced by our contemporaries' and Byron, who with characteristic spleen had written to John Murray of 'the drivelling idiotism of the Mankin' called it 'as sublime as Aeschylus'.

Keats left *Hyperion* incomplete: he was to return to it again. It was included in the 1820 volume with a statement not authorized by Keats that that was not the wish of the author, and the word 'fragment' was, and always since has been, attached to it. Keats, after writing the great *Odes* already quoted, turned to *Lamia, Otho the Great*, and *King*

Stephen and after these to the also unfinished 'faery tale' called *The Cap and Bells;* – to these, and to one other, the serene, exquisite *To Autumn*.

He went to Shanklin in July, 1819, being first with 'a very good fellow indeed, a Mr Rice', of whom he wrote on September 17, 1819 that he is 'the most sensible, and even wise man I know,' and then with Brown, and after the latter's coming he worked prodigiously, at *Lamia* alone and at *Otho the Great* in collaboration with Brown.

In his letter of September 18, 1819, to George and Georgiana he calls *Lamia* 'a short poem', adding, 'I am certain there is that sort of fire in it which must take hold of people in some way – give them either pleasant or unpleasant sensation.' He had, undoubtedly, some hopes of its being a success with the public; and he needed success, financial success, despairingly – for his love's sake. He ranked *Lamia* higher than in his modesty he allowed himself to rank poems much more loved; and his hopes were unfulfilled, both in his lifetime and since. *Lamia* has never been a popular favourite: it is the least read of any of Keats's long poems, less even than *Endymion;* and this is hard judgment – or indifference – for, though it has not the fresh, young enchantment of so much of *Endymion* or the grave, moving beauty of *Hyperion*, its poetic technique is justly rated very high indeed. It may not have 'that sort of fire in it' of which Keats was certain – and he was a remarkably fine critic as well as a great poet – but it has a mastery of the rhymed couplet which was beyond the youthful writer of *Endymion:* in *Endymion* he felt he had 'most likely but moved into the go-cart from the leading strings'. In *Lamia* he is securely planted in independent strength. 'In Lamia,' says Mr M. R. Ridley, 'nothing is more remarkable than the well-proportioned and close-knit articulation of the structure, and the nervous strength of its movement, which makes it easy for it to carry lightly the richness of its adornment.'

Yet the reason for its neglect – apart from the general neglect of all but short poems nowadays – is inherent in its story: that has in it – as it is presented by Keats – what Sir Sidney Colvin, no mean judge and one whose devotion to Keats is incontestable, felt to be a 'fundamental flaw'.

The story is not an intricate one: it is taken from Philostratus and narrated by Burton in his *Anatomy of Melancholy*. It is not clear how long it had been in Keats's mind, but it clearly appealed strongly to his Grecian sense. Lamia is a serpent who takes on the form of a human maiden, beguiles Lycius and calls into being by her witchcraft a house, furniture and so forth and is only discovered at the bridal party by old Apollonius, the sophist, Lycius's instructor – whereupon 'with a frightful scream she vanishes'. As far as this plot is concerned, Keats's poem is straightforward with none of the labyrinthine divagations of *Endymion;* but throughout it is not possible to tell whether the reader is or is not intended to be in sympathy with Lamia and the uncertainty is ruinous.

This is the first description of her:

> She was a gordian shape of dazzling hue,
> Vermilion-spotted, golden, green, and blue;
> Striped like a zebra, freckled like a pard,
> Eyed like a peacock, and all crimson barr'd;
> And full of silver moons, that, as she breath'd,
> Dissolved, or brighter shone, or interwreathed
> Their lustres with the gloomier tapestries –

And this her prayer to Hermes:

SUNSET

I was a woman, let me have once more
A woman's shape, and charming as before.
I love a youth of Corinth — O the bliss!
Give me my woman's form, and place me where he is.
Stoop, Hermes, let me breathe upon thy brow,
And thou shalt see thy sweet nymph even now.

And so, after meeting Lycius, ignoring the one descent into outgrown bad taste in lines 328-332 of Book I, to the wonderful lines than which, as Palgrave has said, 'as mere truthful description, nothing, probably, can be found more true to Hellenic life:'

As men talk in a dream, so Corinth all,
Throughout her palaces imperial,
And all her populous streets and temples lewd,
Mutter'd like tempest in the distance brew'd,
To the wide-spreaded night above her towers.
Men, women, rich and poor, in the cool hours,
Shuffled their sandals o'er the pavement white,
Companion'd or alone; while many a light
Flared, here and there, from wealthy festivals,
And threw their moving shadows on the walls,
Or found them clustering in the corniced shade
Of some arch'd temple door, or dusky colonnade.

There is similar wonder of poetic description in the account of the marriage feast, but at the climax of the story there is the reversion to the discussion with Lamb which originated at Haydon's 'immortal dinner' of December 28, 1817 in this passage:

JOHN KEATS: THE PRINCIPLE OF BEAUTY

> *Do not all charms fly*
> *At the mere touch of cold philosophy?*
> *There was an awful rainbow once in heaven:*
> *We know her woof, her texture; she is given*
> *In the dull catalogue of common things.*
> *Philosophy will clip an Angel's wings,*
> *Conquer all mysteries by rule and line,*
> *Empty the haunted air, and gnomed mine –*
> *Unweave a rainbow, as it erewhile made*
> *The tender-person'd Lamia melt into a shade.*

These lines are completely upsetting: if philosophy is 'cold' – and Apollonius is actually called 'cruel' – and Lamia 'tender-person'd', and melting 'into a shade', the meaning is wholly changed and the interest gone.

However that may be, let us be grateful for the splendour of the poetry. But it is not left as poetry, in the opinion of some. It is with reference particularly to *Lamia* that Mr Middleton Murry passes most definitely from the realm of critical appreciation into that of imaginative supposition: he dislikes Fanny Brawne with such intensity of injustice that he will freely fasten anything deleterious upon her. This is what he has written: 'Lamia, as Keats wrote it, is imaginative autobiography, and of the most exact and faithful kind. Keats is Lycius, Fanny Brawne is the Lamia, and Apollonius is Charles Brown the realist, trying to break Fanny's spell over Keats by insisting upon her as the female animal. The identification seems transparent'.

Of course it may be so: stranger things have happened – but not often. It is speculation undisguised; and contrary, quite, to everything we know of, and love in, Keats as well as opposed to the characters both of Fanny and of Brown.

SUNSET

> *How smiles he at a generation rank'd*
> *In gloomy noddings over Life?*

asks George Meredith of Shakespeare. Delicious as Keats's sense of humour was, it is improbable that this 'identification' would have caused him to smile: it is far more likely that it would have caused him great pain and created in him a keener resentment than ever was created by the assailants in *Blackwood's* and *the Quarterly*. It is true that it is Keats who writes to Bailey on November 22, 1817, that he is certain of nothing but two things and one of them was 'the truth of Imagination': but the other is 'the holiness of the Heart's affections'. He adds, 'What the imagination seizes as Beauty must be truth' – he never wrote, said, or thought that what the imagination seizes as ugliness must be truth. On the contrary, the conclusion of the *Ode on a Grecian Urn* exists to emphasize for all time his real belief.

There is nothing even in the most feverish of the letters written in illness to suggest that Keats ever thought of Fanny as a Lamia or regarded Brown as an Apollonius: he loved Fanny passionately to his life's end; he had his irritations and even jealousies of Brown, but as the last two letters he ever wrote exist to prove, he loved Brown to the end also: 'I cannot bear the sight of any handwriting of a friend I love so much as I do you,' he writes in his final letter, November 30, 1820. Is that to be taken as without sincerity? If so, why? Mr Murry has called Keats 'one of the wisest of men': no man can be justly called wise at all who chooses his love unworthily and lampoons his friends: Keats did neither.

This, in my opinion at least, is as certain as anything can conceivably be, that if it had ever crossed Keats's mind for one single instant that such an 'identification' would ever be made, one year or a hundred years or more after, he – the most generous and loyal-hearted of men – would have destroyed his poem without hesitation. What is really puzzling is that the critic to whom such an 'identification is apparent' should fail to see that by it he belittles the genius – and besmirches the heart – of the poet he undeniably so greatly loves. Moreover, if Keats did, in fact, represent Brown as Apollonius seeking to separate him as Lycius from Fanny as Lamia, then one thing can be asserted beyond any possibility of correction and that is that each of the last two letters of Keats's life, both to Brown, make nonsense – which is not Keats's way, even in the darkest despair of disease. Is it to be supposed that it is in savage irony that he so unbosoms himself to Brown about his thoughts of Fanny and ends the first of these two most poignant letters, 'God bless her, and her mother, and my sister, and George, and his wife, and you, and all!' Brown is here included in the dearest of Keats's dying heart – and we are asked to believe in the 'identification' after this. I, for one, find that wholly fantastic, utterly out of character, and incredible.

During this summer of 1819 Keats was at work, with quite abnormal energy, not only at *Lamia* but also at a play. 'I have finished the Act (Act I, that is) and in the interval of beginning the 2d have proceeded pretty well with Lamia, finishing the 1st part,' he writes to Reynolds on July 12, 1819 – which, again, is a very singular duality if he were, in truth, then at odds with Brown, his collaborator in the play. It is customary to treat his writing of *Otho The Great* as though it were of no importance whatsoever, in part, perhaps, because it is certainly not at all up to the supremely high level of his poems of this great year, and, in part, because it was written in rather a strange way, Brown

SUNSET

supplying the plot and Keats writing the dialogue; moreover, Keats wrote that, as directed, scene by scene, without knowing – so Brown said – what was to follow, until he revolted from any collaboration so unnatural, demanded to know the proposed conclusion, rejected some of Brown's suggestions, and wrote Act V on his own lines.

It is true that Keats said he was 'only acting as midwife' to Brown's plot; but it is really asking too much of our understanding for us to be left to suppose that the two friends lodging together did not in these circumstances constantly discuss the play from which they hoped 'to share moderate Profits', and indeed Keats's own words are inconsistant with such an understanding: on July 31, 1819, for instance, Keats writes to Dilke, 'Brown and I are pretty well harnessed again to our dog-cart. I mean the Tragedy which goes on sinkingly – we are thinking of introducing an Elephant', and so on.

The two friends 'removed to Winchester for the convenience of a Library', as Keats tells Bailey on August 14, adding a brief account of his quite astounding literary activity: four acts of the play were then completed and whilst busy on Act V Keats could write to Taylor, 'I feel every confidence that if I choose I may be a popular writer', though he at once adds, 'that I will never be; but for all that I will get a livelihood'.

Was ever any young writer, especially one poor and in love, not torn between desire to earn and the pangs of fame? Keats and Brown had every hope that their play would be produced by Kean, but unhappily Kean went off to America. Keats, having finished it and finished *Lamia*, occupied himself in September, 1819, 'in revising St Agnes' Eve and studying Italian'.

Keats's own opinion, written to George and Georgiana,

JOHN KEATS: THE PRINCIPLE OF BEAUTY

JOHN KEATS: THE PRINCIPLE OF BEAUTY

JOHN KEATS: THE PRINCIPLE OF BEAUTY

JOHN KEATS: THE PRINCIPLE OF BEAUTY

JOHN KEATS: THE PRINCIPLE OF BEAUTY

was that *Otho The Great* was 'a tolerable tragedy'; but he was characteristically philosophical over his disappointment; 'I feel', he wrote, 'I can bear real ills better than imaginary ones' – in which he is not alone. No one now reads *Otho The Great*, and it has never been acted. And yet, though it is melodramatic and involved, it is Keats's writing, contemporary with his greatest work, and, accordingly, singularly neglected. Here is a brief extract, Otho, Emperor of Germany meeting Auranthe, sister to Conrad, Duke of Franconia:

> *Hail my sweet hostess! I do thank the stars,*
> *Or my good soldiers, or their ladies' eyes,*
> *That, after such a merry battle fought,*
> *I can, all safe in body and in soul,*
> *Kiss your fair hand and lady Fortune's too.*
> *My ring! Now, on my life, it doth rejoice*
> *These lips to feel 't on this soft ivory!*
> *Keep it, my brightest daughter; it may prove*
> *The little prologue to a line of Kings.*
> *I strove against thee and my hot-blood son,*
> *Dull blockhead that I was to be so blind,*
> *But now my sight is clear; forgive me, lady.*
> *Auranthe: My lord, I was a vassal to your frown,*
> *And now your favour makes me but more humble;*
> *In wintry winds the simple snow is safe,*
> *But fadeth at the greeting of the sun:*
> *Unto thine anger I might well have spoken,*
> *Taking on me a woman's privilege,*
> *But this so sudden kindness makes me dumb.*

It is neither Shakespeare nor the Keats of *Hyperion*; but it